Wicked EDISTO

THE DARK SIDE OF EDEN

ALEXIA JONES HELSLEY

THE
History
PRESS

Published by The History Press
Charleston, SC 29403
www.historypress.net

Copyright © 2014 by Alexia Jones Helsley
All rights reserved

Cover images of Andrew G. Magrath and Daniel Chamberlain courtesy of the South
Carolina Department of Archives and History.

First published 2014

Manufactured in the United States

ISBN 978.1.62619.234.8

Library of Congress CIP data applied for.

Notice: The information in this book is true and complete to the best of our knowledge. It is
offered without guarantee on the part of the author or The History Press. The author and
The History Press disclaim all liability in connection with the use of this book.

All rights reserved. No part of this book may be reproduced or transmitted in any form
whatsoever without prior written permission from the publisher except in the case of brief
quotations embodied in critical articles and reviews.

Dedicated to H/P Crew
Blessings abound

Then God said, "Let the waters below the heavens be gathered into one place, and let the dry land appear"; and it was so. God called the dry land earth, and the gathering of the waters He called seas; and God saw that it was good.
Genesis 1:9-10 (NASB)

Contents

Contents

Preface

E disto Island is a palimpsest of human habitation—a picturesque mix of marsh and live oaks, dense vegetation, winding creeks and wildlife with a sliver of beach washed by the Atlantic. For thousands of years, men have sought opportunity beneath the live oaks. Prehistoric men lived along the waterways, paddled dugouts along the shoreline and left shell rings and pottery shards as mute evidence of their existence.

Botany Bay, December 2012. *Jacob Helsley, photographer.*

In historic times, Europeans and Africans contended with the original inhabitants for this verdant land. Some found adventure pursuing dreams of wealth and opportunity; others created settlements and agricultural oases in the semitropical wilderness; and still others met disappointment and death. But all faced challenges of natural disasters, external threats, disease, daily uncertainties, adapting to new surroundings and the evil that lurks in the hearts of men.

Acknowledgements

I gratefully acknowledge the assistance of Chad Rhoad and Katie Parry of The History Press; Beth Bilderback, visual materials archivist, and Henry Fulmer, director, of the South Caroliniana Library; Karen L. Carter of the Edisto Bookstore; Herb J. Hartsook, director, and Kate Moore, archivist, South Carolina Political Collections, Hollings Special Collections Library, University of South Carolina; and Steve Tuttle, director of reference services, Brian Collars and Marion Chandler, archivists, of the South Carolina Department of Archives and History.

Special thanks to Terry Helsley, my husband, indexer, editor and photographer, and to Jacob Helsley for sharing his photographic views of Edisto.

Island Paradise

Historical Overview

Crossing the bridge, one enters a primordial world of salt marsh, waterfowl and crustaceans—as Samuel Taylor Coleridge wrote, "water, water, everywhere." To the visitor, this is a quiet place, a calm refuge, an escape from the hurly-burly of work, commutes and deadlines. Many echo the thoughts of an 1865 visitor: "It seemed like fairy land—everything so fresh and green—the air so soft." But to the long-term resident, it is a place of nuanced beauty where rip currents trawl the coastline and human emotions and misadventures mar the tranquil scene.

Edisto Island lies roughly forty miles to the southeast of Charleston. The landscape hugs the earth; the clouds are low, and egrets daintily pick their way through the marsh. The North Edisto and Dawhoo Rivers and the Intracoastal Waterway bound the island to the north and northeast, the South Edisto lies to the southwest and the Atlantic Ocean is the island's southeast boundary. Cut by creeks and marshes, Edisto is many islands, such as Little Edisto, Scanawah, Edisto Beach and Bailey's.

Modern Edisto reflects the long interface of man and nature—Native American villages and fields, the planter and his black workers wresting indigo and sea-island cotton from an alien land, dangerous work that shaped master and slave. Roads follow ancient paths. Beach walkers find pottery shards, chunks of handmade brick and slivers of fossilized mammoth ivory.

During Edisto's long history, invaders—Spanish, Indian, British and Union—disturbed the rhythms of daily life, tracing their letters in the sand.

Store Creek with egret, Edisto Island, July 2013. *Terry Helsley, photographer.*

Sea oats, Edisto Beach, July 2013. *Terry Helsley, photographer.*

Temporary visitors or long-term residents—all defy nature, brave storms and dance ancient waltzes of death, destruction and decay.

To a degree, Edisto's written story begins in 1666, when English explorer Robert Sandford published an account of his exploration of the Carolina coast. In *A Relation of a Voyage on the Coast of the Province of Carolina*, Sandford described sailing up the North Edisto. The tide was at "halfe Ebbe," and about four or five miles inland, Sandford anchored and met a canoe with two Native Americans. The natives boarded the ship and identified the area as the "Country of Edistoh." Their chief town—the seat of the cassique (chief)—lay on the western shore of the island toward the ocean. Sandford described shoals, bluffs and breakers with hammocks "of thicke shrubby trees." Sandford's natural landmarks still define the island today. His seventeenth-century landscape resonates with modern visitors.

Killers and Marauders

"*Trouble in Paradise*"

Early Edisto was a beautiful but dangerous place. Settlers faced an inhospitable environment, resentful native inhabitants, disgruntled slave workers and foreign raiders. The easy water access made Edisto an inviting target. Also, the English were not the first Europeans to visit Edisto. Based on explorations of Hernando de Soto, Lucas Vazquez de Ayllon and others, the Spanish crown claimed the Carolina Lowcountry. During the sixteenth century, the Spaniards established a fort and provincial capital on Parris Island. But in 1587, the Spanish forces withdrew from Carolina to consolidate their position at St. Augustine. Although the Spaniards destroyed their settlement, Santa Elena on Parris Island, and relocated the settlers, they still claimed the land for the Spanish king. So, well into the eighteenth century, the Spaniards and their black and Indian allies continued to raid the Carolina Lowcountry, destroying crops and livestock, burning homes, terrorizing residents and disrupting the slave workforce. Even one hundred years later, the Spaniards still considered the English settlers as interlopers who had settled illegally in Spanish territory.

In 1686, Spanish forces launched their deadliest raid on the Carolina Lowcountry. The Spaniards seemed invincible until one of those proverbial acts of God. A major hurricane not only overwhelmed the survivors on Edisto and Port Royal Islands but also destroyed two of the three Spanish galleys and sent the survivors and the last galley back to St. Augustine. In the end, the Spanish attack was deadly for those the raiders encountered but not lethal for the survival of the young colony because, thanks to a providential storm, the capital of Charles Towne was spared.

THE ATTACK ON STUART TOWN AND ENVIRONS

Antagonism between English and Spanish ran deep, and peaceful coexistence was tenuous at best. In the 1680s, newcomers—European and Indian—exacerbated the situation. In 1685, a group of Highland Scots settled at Stuart Town near Beaufort. These highlanders built homes, developed farm and pasture lands, erected fences and feuded with colonial officials in Charles Towne. They challenged the status quo by inserting themselves into the lucrative Indian trade and agitating the recently arrived Yemassee, a large group of Native Americans who had fled Spanish Florida and settled in ten towns—with names such as Yemassee, Poca Sabo, Okatie and Huspah—in Old Beaufort District.

Encouraged by their new "friends" and trading associates, the Yemassee raided Spanish-held La Florida, destroying the villages of Indians loyal to the Spaniards and selling their inhabitants as slaves. As a result, incensed by the activities of these highlanders and their Indian allies, at least one hundred Spaniards with their African and Indian allies attacked and destroyed Stuart Town, Beaufort and outlying plantations on Port Royal Island. Not only did troops destroy houses and outbuildings, but they also burned fields and killed and scattered livestock and human settlers. After several days of pillaging and destruction, the Spaniards with their human prisoners left the Beaufort area and moved on to Edisto Island. There, the raiders—according to Major William Dunlop, five hundred men (other sources suggest one hundred) on "2 or 3 great ships"—ravaged the island and environs and destroyed the property of two provincial officials: Joseph Morton and Paul Grimball.

At the time of the raid, Joseph Morton was the governor of South Carolina. He served two terms as governor, from 1682 to 1684 and from 1685 to 1686. The Spanish raiders forced their way into the Morton residence and ransacked it. They kidnapped his brother-in-law, Edward Bowell, stole all of Morton's money and silver plate and also "liberated" thirteen slaves. After assessing the situation, Morton valued his material losses at £1,500 sterling.

PAUL GRIMBALL

Arriving on August 24, 1686, the Spaniards and their black and Indian allies spent five days at the compound and plantation of Paul Grimball "wasting killing & destroying" Grimball's home, possessions, cattle and workforce. At the time, Grimball was in Charles Towne. After Grimball visited the scene of

Edisto Island from *Carte Particuliere de la Caroline*, circa 1696. This early map shows the location of Paul Grimball's property on the island. *Courtesy of South Carolina Department of Archives and History*.

desolation, he compiled and, later, submitted a lengthy list of losses including three despoiled houses, burned fences, at least sixteen head of cattle killed and many more so frightened that cowherds could never lure them from the woods. The Spaniards also abducted thirteen slaves and Kate Oats, an English servant in the Grimball household. According to William Dunlop (soldier, chaplain and government official), the enemies left "severall Markes of his Malice especially the half burnt body of one of our people."

Paul Grimball was an English merchant who arrived in South Carolina in 1682. He acquired land on the Cooper River and, later in 1683, received a grant from the proprietors for 1,590 acres on Edisto Island. Grimball settled on Edisto Island and developed a large complex, including a main house and outbuildings. Grimball, a prominent member of the new colony, held a number of important provincial offices: proprietor's deputy, secretary of the province, receiver general and escheator. He later ran afoul of provincial politics and was temporarily removed from office and even imprisoned in 1691.

According to Grimball, before dawn on February 3, 1691, Constable William Chapman of Charles Towne and seven others, "armed with clubs" and allegedly searching for public records formerly in Grimball's custody (in his role as secretary of the province), stormed his Edisto home. The men not only ransacked the house but also terrorized Grimball's wife and family. Not content with disrupting the Grimball household, Chapman also led his posse to the home of Grimball's son-in-law, John Hamilton (husband of Grimball's daughter Mary), and similarly mistreated Hamilton's family. Yet the resilient Grimball survived the physical and political attacks and, in time, regained his position. In recognition of the confidence the proprietors (who owned and governed the colony of South Carolina until 1719) had in Grimball, in April 1693, they also granted Grimball the authority to designate and remove colonial sheriffs and judges. When Grimball made his will in 1696, he styled himself as "Paul Grimball, Esq: of Edisto Island."

CHARLES ODINGSELL

The Grimball family's penchant for unusual situations resurfaced in the third generation. In 1741, Paul Grimball's grandson Charles Odingsell died in unusual circumstances. Odingsell was the son of Ann Grimball, daughter of Mary and Paul Grimball, and her second husband, Charles Odingsell. Under Grimball, the older Charles Odingsell was deputy secretary of the province of South Carolina. Odingsell, the son of Ann and Charles, married Sarah Livingston. During a visit to nearby Savannah, Georgia, Odingsell left his lodging during the night. While walking the city streets, a law officer mistook him for a "stroller" (a loafer or idler) and seized him. He was taken to the guardhouse without any legal proceedings, and there officers threatened Odingsell with confinement in the stocks and a trip to the whipping post. According to contemporary accounts, "the Terror and Fright" of his experience so traumatized him that Odingsell developed a high fever. Once he was freed from confinement, friends carried Odingsell to his boat. Unfortunately, en route home, the poor man died "aboard his Boat" near Daufuskie Island. Odingsell was buried in Savannah. According to his tombstone, he was only fifty-six years old at the time of his death.

AFTERMATH

On August 17, 1686, three Spanish galleys loaded with loot "sailed northward" from Stuart Town and Edisto toward Charles Towne. General Thomas DeLeon commanded the Spanish military force and the company of Native Americans that accompanied them. The threat to the capital

Spanish caravel *Santa Maria*. The arrival of the Spaniards and their ships spread fear along the South Carolina coast. *Courtesy of Library of Congress, Prints & Photographs Division, Detroit Publishing Company Collection, LC-D4-21178.*

was serious. The Spaniards had the manpower and firepower to destroy the city. Nevertheless, providence intervened. A major hurricane struck the coast of South Carolina. Winds intercepted and wrecked the Spanish fleet before the galleys reached Charles Towne. DeLeon commanded the Spanish flagship *Rosario*. During the hurricane, the flagship ran aground and DeLeon drowned. Another galley "breached and burned." Unfortunately, Governor Morton's brother-in-law burned to death in the second ship. In the end, only one of the three Spanish raiders limped home to St. Augustine.

THE YEMASSEE WAR

Despite surviving the Spanish incursion in 1686, the ensuing decades were times of uncertainty and disquietude. The Yemassee War of 1715–16 was a major threat to the survival of the colony. On Good Friday 1715, Yemassee seized and murdered negotiators, Indian traders and their families in their Lowcountry towns. Only the escape of Seymour Burroughs from Pocotaligo saved the inhabitants of Port Royal Island. The frightened residents boarded a ship in the harbor at Beaufort and sailed for Charles Town. The settlers between Port Royal and Charles Town were not as fortunate. With no warning, Yemassee and their Indian allies fell on unsuspecting settlements and, for example, killed almost one hundred in Granville and hundreds in Colleton County. Learning of the attack, the South Carolina governor hastily summoned militiamen from Edisto, John's and James Island to oppose the Indian attack. The Yemassee War was the greatest Indian threat faced by any of the thirteen colonies. The Yemassee, Creek and other Indian groups united in this effort to push the European settlers out of South Carolina. The Indian warriors killed hundreds of settlers along the Edisto and Combahee Rivers. Frightened settlers fled to Charles Town, and as a result, the area south of the Stono River was virtually unoccupied. The colony rallied with assistance from Massachusetts and eventually negotiated a treaty with the Creek. The Yemassee abandoned their South Carolina towns and retreated south to Florida. A total of 7 percent of the colony's white population died during the war. Slowly, the colony regained its direction, and in time, the settlers returned to Edisto, Port Royal and other abandoned Sea Islands. Recovery, however, was slow.

In response to this Indian alliance that involved all major Indian groups in the Southeast except the Cherokee, South Carolina's leaders organized for defense and established outposts and scout boats to patrol the colony's waterways between Charles Town and Florida. These efforts continued for years. For example, in 1740, the Commons House of Assembly was still funding men such as John Devant, William Conyers and Joseph Wilcox for their service stationed "at the Look Out on North Edistoe Inlet." In addition, a committee on "Security and Defences of the province" recommended to the assembly certain measures, including:

> *That the Owners of Slaves on Wadmelaw [sic] and Edisto Islands, and in all other Parts of the Province of the Distance of (or exceeding) 40 Miles from Charles Town, be obliged to employ every 5th able male Slave to work for a Week together in erecting Forts on the Frontiers in certain Places to be directed by the Law for that Purpose.*

The Edisto militia was also involved in the 1740 expedition against St. Augustine. To many South Carolinians, there was no safety as long as the Spanish held St. Augustine. Life for island residents remained uncertain. In 1753, according to the *South Carolina Gazette*, two Native Americans murdered an unnamed settler and her children on Edisto Island.

According to historian Lawrence Sanders, in the spring of 1763, as the Seven Years' War (1756–63) wound to an end, the "last of the Spanish privateers interrupted South Carolina commerce." Don Martin, commanding the *Santa Maria*, sailed from St. Augustine toward South Carolina. Near Port Royal, they captured a brigantine. Later, Martin and his force landed and plundered a plantation near Edisto.

Friends and Foes

The American Revolution was South Carolina's first civil war. Brothers fought brothers, and Patriot and Loyalist militia ravaged each other's settlements, ambushed foraging parties, tortured women, murdered opponents and burned homes and farms. Violence and uncertainty plagued the Carolina homefront. Though removed from major scenes of action, even Edisto Island experienced death and disloyalty. In the early years of the war, the South Carolina Lowcountry was a quiet place. After the South Carolinians successfully rebuffed the British at Fort Moultrie on Sullivan's Island in 1776, Carolinians relaxed and enjoyed the calm, and fervor for the war effort waned.

But the lull did not last. By 1778, the British had launched their vaunted southern strategy. The British high command sent Colonel Augustine Prevost to develop a staging area for attacking Savannah and Charles Town. The British goal was to conquer the southern colonies one by one and literally roll up American resistance and crush Washington's forces between the British-controlled Middle Atlantic States and the South. The British also expected great support for their military effort from southern Loyalists. Prevost established his headquarters at Beaufort, and on December 20, 1778, British forces seized control of Savannah and occupied the South Carolina Lowcountry. Yet despite British inroads, General Benjamin Lincoln, commander of the Continental army, did not surrender Charles Town to the British until 1780.

JAMES MURRAY, REVOLUTIONARY SOLDIER

According to the journal of Brigadier Major Francis Skelly, a British officer, on June 26, 1779, the first division of British forces crossed to Edisto Island. The following day, Lieutenant Colonel John Maitland and the last British division also arrived on the island. As a result, the "whole army [was] on that Island." The presence of this British force demonstrates the vulnerability of Edisto Island during the American Revolution.

Murray was a Patriot and supported American independence. In January 1775, the "committee appointed to carry into effect the Continental Association" named Murray as a member for Edisto. The association was a response to British taxes and tariffs. Individuals who signed the association agreed not to import British goods until the British Parliament repealed the offending acts. On October 2, 1775, Murray enlisted in the Edisto Island Militia under Captain Joseph Jenkins. In that same month, Captain Jenkins wrote the Council of Safety requesting gunpowder for the militia companies on Edisto Island. On October 13, Henry Laurens, president of the Council of Safety, answered Jenkins, directing him to secure gunpowder from the Colleton Regiment and noting that "the Council of Safety will order four four-pound Cannon together with a proper quantity of Corn Powder to be delivered to Jenkins for the service you point out." Murray represented the Parish of St. John, Colleton, in the South Carolina House of Representatives. According to one of Murray's descendants, Murray died from a cannon explosion in 1779 "while defending the Island." Murray, who had married Abigail Jenkins, is buried in the Jenkins family cemetery on Edisto Island.

From the memoirs of General William Moultrie, in February 1779, following the Battle of Beaufort, privateers from the HMS *Vigilant* "burned all the plantations along Skull Creek on Hilton Head and Pinckney Islands. They also sailed into St. Helena Sound and attacked Edisto Island, causing the death of James Murray, a member of the General Assembly, when the Edisto militia cannon exploded." The *Gazette of the State of South Carolina* confirmed Murray's death on February 2, 1779: "killed in action on Edisto Island."

As the British prepared for the siege of Charles Town in 1780, their navy was busy in the Edisto area. Captain Peter Russell and his men reconnoitered the island and reported on February 13, 1780, possibly with an eye for resupply, that there were five hundred horses, two thousand sheep and two thousand cattle on the island. On February 14, several residents of the island approached Russell and asked for protection from the British. In turn, Russell ordered them to collect "Government Horses" on the island and drive them

The cannon beside Edisto Realty, December 2013. Dated 1765, this is one of two colonial-era cannons found on Edisto. *Terry Helsley, photographer.*

to the landing. The residents honored their commitment and delivered eight horses to the British. Yet all was not well, and on February 18, residents registered complaints that the sailors had plundered their homes and stolen or killed their livestock. On February 26, Russell also sent sick and injured British troops to convalesce at the Jenkins House on Edisto.

ISLAND LOYALISTS

When Charles Town surrendered to the British in 1780, the British plan to conquer the southern states and pressure General George Washington to surrender seemed to be working. On May 12, Major General Benjamin Lincoln surrendered a fighting force of over five thousand, including the Continental troops under his command. The British occupied South Carolina's capital, Charles Town, and turned their attention to securing the rest of the state. Unfortunately for the Patriot cause, when word of the debacle spread, commanders of inland installations also surrendered their forts and troops to the British. The British were confident that South Carolina was once again a British possession and anticipated military support from Crown supporters in the state.

Surrender of Lord Cornwallis. *John Trumball, artist. Library of Congress, Prints and Photographs Division, LC-DIG-det-4a26441.*

After the fall of Charles Town, the British controlled the seat of government. Many state leaders, including three signers of the Declaration of Independence, were in British hands. The victorious British imprisoned some Patriot leaders but paroled many others. In order to return home to their families, many of these former Patriot supporters accepted parole, took British protection and agreed not to take up arms against the British. To many who had once espoused the Patriot cause, it appeared that the independence effort was lost, and they only wanted to return to their homes, families and livelihoods. Some even accepted British military commissions or held civil positions, such as justice of the peace or parish commissioner. But the Patriot forces regrouped under leaders such as Thomas Sumter and Francis Marion and waged an effective guerrilla campaign against British forces and their allies in South Carolina. Later, with the assistance of the new Continental commander, General Nathanael Greene, "the fighting Quaker," Patriots regained control of the state. As General Cornwallis withdrew from South Carolina, he marched toward Yorktown, Virginia, to await reinforcements. Instead, his world "turned upside down," and with his defeat and surrender, American independence was assured.

In 1782, the South Carolina legislature met in Jacksonboro for the first time since the fall of Charles Town. Among other items of business, it passed legislation confiscating or amercing (taxing) the lands of many of the Loyalists. In addition, the legislators banished some of the Loyalists from the state. According to the 1782 act, there were several classes of confiscations. One class, for example, affected individuals who had taken British commissions or held civil office under the British; another covered those who had signed an address to Sir Henry Clinton and Admiral Mariot Arbuthnot after the fall of Charles Town in 1780; another affected individuals who had congratulated General Charles Cornwallis on his victory at Camden; and another was simply titled "Obnoxious Persons." Affected individuals, their families and heirs spent years petitioning the South Carolina General Assembly for relief from the provisions of the act. Some regained their lands or had their amercements reduced or lifted. Others, such as former lieutenant governor William Bull of Sheldon, did not.

The Confiscation Acts affected several prominent Edisto Island planters and their families. For example, the acts included planters such as Joseph Seabrook, William Meggett and Isaac Rippon. To secure their property and protect their positions, Meggett, Rippon and Seabrook petitioned the South Carolina General Assembly for relief.

JOSEPH SEABROOK

Joseph Seabrook Sr. (1720–1790) was a native of Edisto Island and a pre-Revolutionary civic leader. Prior to the war, he served as a justice of the peace, and in 1770, he was appointed a commissioner for building a chapel of ease "at some convenient place" on Edisto Island in St. John Parish, Colleton County. According to historian Kathy Roe Coker, Seabrook owned at least 596 acres of land on the island. In his petition for relief, Seabrook defended his actions after the fall of Charles Town. For example, he contended that "during the late troubles," he preferred to remain "peaceably at home." But as that was not his destiny, he made the best of the situation. As a mitigating circumstance for his actions, he cited the lawless condition of Edisto Island, alleging that the area was "much infected by plundering." As a result, according to Seabrook, in order to prevent additional "distress," after the fall of Charles Town, his neighbors pressured him to accept a British commission. Apparently, the residents of Edisto Island thought any military presence—regardless of allegiance—was better than none. In one of his petitions, Seabrook also candidly acknowledged "that after the Capitulation [fall of Charles Town] he like many others took a British protection for the preservation of his property & benefit of his family."

The general assembly committee that investigated Seabrook's claims found evidence to support his allegations. According to its report, the sixty-three-year-old Seabrook did not seek his commission as a captain of the Edisto Island loyal militia. Rather, although he preferred to remain quietly on his plantations, the inhabitants of Edisto Island unanimously requested and urged Seabrook to accept the commission in order to maintain public order and prevent additional plundering of the island's residents. As a result of these mitigating circumstances, which it verified, the committee recommended that Seabrook be relieved from confiscation. Seabrook also asserted his firm attachment to the "interest of America." Nevertheless, the committee wanted Seabrook's lands amerced "for the use of the State as some Atonement for his Misbehaviour [*sic*] in accepting a Commission from the Enemy or any pretence [*sic*] whatever." In 1784, the South Carolina General Assembly accepted the committee's recommendation but also prohibited Seabrook from ever again holding public office. Seabrook's defense not only aided his quest for relief from the Confiscation Acts but also raised issues about the morale and core sentiments of island residents.

While there may have been extenuating circumstances surrounding Seabrook's involvement with the Loyalist militia, that was not the case with his son, Captain Joseph Seabrook Jr. (1750–1831). The younger Seabrook was an active Tory and married for the second time Martha Deveaux in Nassau in 1789. Seabrook accepted a British commission and perhaps held office after the fall of Charles Town. His property was confiscated under the first Confiscation Act, but the penalty was later reduced. The younger Seabrook's property was instead amerced at 12 percent. According to the 1800 census, both Joseph Seabrook Sr. and Jr. lived in South Carolina, so neither had been banished.

ISAAC RIPPON AND WILLIAM MEGGETT

Isaac Rippon, born on John's Island, was one of forty-eight persons whose property was amerced by the original legislation. William Meggett was a native of St. Helena Parish. In 1784, Rippon asked to be "relieved from the penalties of Amercement Act passed at Jacksonburgh." He noted that he had earlier petitioned for relief in a previous session. At that time, his petition was turned down because there were "no representatives" from his home parish serving in the House. Consequently, there was no one to vouch for him. Since that situation had changed, Rippon reapplied. He now had witnesses who were aware of his "warmest attachment to the freedom of America" and that he had never offended one of his countrymen. Rippon admitted that he served as a justice under the British but "only to exempt himself from Militia duty."

In February 1783, William Meggett also petitioned for relief from the Amercement Act. In his petition to the House of Representatives, Meggett stated that he was "entirely unconscious of any part of his conduct, but that of being a Militia Officer during the British Government [that] could be deemed criminal." Odd wording, perhaps, as what could be more egregious than accepting an enemy commission during war? He continued that although he held a British commission, "he shewed [sic] every mark of Indulgence and treated the American prisoners on the island, with humanity and politeness." From Meggett's comments, it is clear that at times, the British held American prisoners on Edisto Island.

RESOLUTION

Finally, in March 1785, after years of petitioning, a committee of the South Carolina House of Representatives recommended that Rippon, Meggett and others be released from the "Operation of the Law." In addition, a committee to investigate the conduct of Alexander Chisolm, Isaac Rippon, James Clark and Joseph Seabrook reported that all "were always deemed respectable Citizens, much esteemed by their Neighours [sic]." Rippon's and Meggett's long waits for redemption ended. Interestingly, their prewar respectability trumped their actions during the last months of the war.

Cat among the Pigeons

Following the American Revolution, the state was devastated and its economy in tatters. South Carolinians faced daunting challenges as they worked to rebuild their shattered lives. Many had lost family members, and there were hundreds of widows and orphans, many of whom faced tenuous futures with few resources. Veterans coped with injuries, wounds and long-term health issues. South Carolinians had lost homes, livestock, laborers, stores, taverns, places of worship, stock in trade and family members. Although generally on the fringes of the war, Edisto Island was not exempt from the devastation of war or immune to the economic and personal distress of the postwar years.

As early as 1779, British forces were on the island. This incursion possibly resulted in the death of James Murray. Later, in 1782, Colonel Edward Lacey and South Carolina militiamen clashed with British forces on Edisto Island. Following the fall of Charles Town, some residents had sought British protection—perhaps to end civil unrest on the island or to return to their families—and by 1782, even the Patriot militiamen were disenchanted with the new state government. William Hardin, a noted Patriot militia leader, was passed over for promotion. In a time of divided loyalties and political ambiguities, residents faced economic issues as well: workers were gone (some slaves sought freedom behind British lines), livestock was lost or stolen, crops were destroyed and the lucrative British indigo subsidy was lost. In the late 1780s, with peace declared, residents were coming to grips with a new order.

THE REVEREND BEVERLY ANTHONY ALLEN

Into this challenging, changing world came an unexpected adversary: the Reverend Beverly Anthony Allen. Allen was born in 1757 in Spotsylvania, Virginia. According to Robert Bray, prior to his conversion, Allen was a well-respected physician practicing in Talbot County, Maryland. In 1778, Allen affiliated with a new religious movement, Methodism, and became an itinerant minister. Initially in 1780, Allen was on probationary status, but by 1782, he was a full-fledged Methodist minister. At first, Allen preached in Maryland, but later he was active preaching the new faith in Georgia and the Carolinas and even introduced Methodism into Salisbury, North Carolina.

Of special interest for the history of Methodism in America, Methodist leaders convened the critically important Christmas Conference in Baltimore, Maryland, in 1784. At this first Methodist conference, attendees elected Francis Asbury and Thomas Coke as their first superintendents (later known as bishops) and organized the denomination as the Methodist Episcopal Church in America. Coke, representing John Wesley in England, then ordained other church leaders such as deacons and presbyters and also consecrated Asbury as superintendent. Also at that time, according to Bray, the new denomination elected Allen one of the "original twelve elders of the new Methodist Episcopal Church" in America. The elders organized circuits to cover vast geographical areas and then assigned men to cover the circuits and administer the sacraments to Methodists wherever they lived. As Allen did not attend the Christmas Conference, Asbury officially ordained him in 1785. In the early formative period of Methodist history, Allen was one of the new denomination's important leaders.

Allen, according to Methodist historian Albert Shipp, was a "man of extraordinary talents." A popular and spellbinding preacher, Allen associated with such Methodist luminaries as Thomas Coke and Francis Asbury and even corresponded with the founder of Methodism, John Wesley. Coke in particular supported Allen's advancement in the denomination. For example, during the famous Christmas Conference, Coke noted in his journal that "Allen was a physician of great eminence in these parts, and a most precious man of excellent sense, and of the greatest simplicity." During his meteoric rise, Allen was even, according to some sources, considered as a possible bishop.

In 1785, Coke and Asbury sent Allen as the first Methodist missionary to Georgia. His circuit covered the entire state—a daunting task. In this pioneer assignment, Allen reported many converts to Methodism. Contemporaries described him "as a brilliant young preacher of striking appearance." As the first Methodist itinerant (traveling minister) in Georgia, he also enjoyed the respect of his ministerial peers. Elbert County, his home, played a prominent role in early Methodist history. Asbury sponsored the Methodist Annual Conference in 1788 at Thompson's Meeting House in Elbert County.

At this juncture, Allen's future looked bright. Regardless of the assignment, he succeeded. Yet these were anxious times as the young denomination charted its course in America. Coke later returned to the British Isles but made several later trips to the United States and in 1785 presented an antislavery petition to President George Washington.

His counterpart, Bishop Asbury, was known as a man of unbending opinions who governed the American church with an iron hand. He and Thomas Coke, known as the father of Methodist missions, often worked at cross purposes and did not always see eye to eye. In addition, some younger ministers chafed under Asbury's firm administration. Allen, the confident rising star, was not afraid to state his positions or differ with Asbury. As Asbury noted, he considered Allen "a promising young man, but a little of a Dissenter." At one point, he even considered Allen a threat to Methodist unity: "Poor Beverly Allen, who has been going from bad to worse these seven or eight years—speaking against me to the preachers and people, and writing to Mr. Wesley and Dr. Coke."

According to the general minutes in 1787, the Methodists elected the charismatic Allen a presiding elder, and from his success in Georgia, the church sent Beverly Allen as a missionary to Charleston. In June 1785, Allen, according to historian John Atkinson, "one of the most commanding preachers of Methodism," began his work in Charleston. As Allen wrote, "The field seemed white unto the harvest" as "the people were ready to hear the word." Also in 1785, Allen established the Great Pee Dee Circuit in North Carolina. According to his account, "Many hundreds flocked to hear the word of the Lord, and many were truly awakened." As Bray observed, Allen was a charismatic preacher with a message that resonated in the early years of the new nation. Hundreds responded to his message of God's grace with its call to repentance and new life.

At first, adherents of the new denomination shared facilities with a Baptist congregation in Charleston. Later, the Methodists moved into the home of a Methodist convert. In time, there were so many followers that the Methodists had to find even larger quarters. Yet the early success of the Methodists also provoked a reaction, as Allen noted, "The people became almost afraid to hear us, lest they should be infected with Methodism, which they deemed as

Bishop Francis Asbury, Methodist Episcopal Church in the United States. At times, Allen and Asbury clashed about church matters. *Benjamin Tanner, engraver, 1814. Library of Congress Prints and Photographs Division. LC-USZC4-6153.*

dangerous as the plague." Despite this opposition, Methodism in Charleston continued to grow so much that when Asbury visited in January 1786, he found a thriving congregation of over thirty ready to begin erecting its own church building on Cumberland Street.

As Allen's professional life prospered, so did his personal life. In February 1786, at Cainhoy in Berkeley County, Allen married Anna Singletary. She was the youngest daughter of John and Sarah Singletary of St. Thomas and St. Denis Parish. John Singletary was a prominent planter who owned a plantation on the Wando River. Allen's bride, one of three sisters, was a devout young woman. Five years later, in April 1791, according to the *Charleston City Gazette*, John Singletary, "an old and respectable gentleman," died of influenza. By his will, Singletary bequeathed fourteen slaves to his daughter Anna Allen and named her, following the death of his wife, the residual heir to his Wando plantation. Beverly Allen was one of the executors of Singletary's estate.

By a few months, John Singletary died before his son-in-law's disgrace. His wife was not as fortunate. Sarah Singletary wrote her will in 1793, and the document reflects her unease about Anna Allen's welfare. When Sarah died in 1798, she specifically left several slaves in trust for her daughter Anna with the stipulation that if she left South Carolina, Singletary's executors would retain the slaves in the state and forward to Anna any income from their labor "for her support and maintenance." If Anna Allen survived her husband, the slaves would become her property. If she died before Beverly Allen, Sarah Singletary left the slaves to Anna's children. The wording of the will suggests a mother's concern for her daughter's future and her disappointment in Beverly Allen.

PRIDE AND A FALL

The year 1791 was an important one for Allen. His father-in-law died, and in May, he completed and mailed a special manuscript to John Wesley. The manuscript was Allen's magnum opus, an account of his success in Georgia and South Carolina. Allen compared himself to Nehemiah as a founder of the temple. To some readers, Allen's account seemed prideful, but Wesley was impressed by what he read. In 1792, Allen's manuscript, titled "Some Account of the Work of God in America," appeared in the *Arminian Magazine*.

In 1791, Coke tapped Allen for a new assignment and sent him as the Methodist missionary to Edisto Island, a place of special interest for Coke. At the time, Coke thought he had the right man for the job and even wrote an associate: "I have now had the pleasure of finding out a very able missionary for Edisto Island, Brother Beverly Allen." Yet as events unfolded, it became clear that Coke's confidence was misplaced.

Allen arrived on the island without a meetinghouse. Possibly, he preached in homes of island residents or perhaps in the local Episcopal Church. What happened on Edisto is a matter of great conjecture. Yet his assignment on Edisto Island was Allen's undoing, as his illustrious career abruptly ended. The Methodist conference minutes for 1792 tersely note opposite Allen's name: "Expelled from the connection: Beverly Allen." Ironically, by the time Allen's personal account of his ministry appeared in print, he was no longer a Methodist missionary.

There is little concrete information about what transpired on Edisto Island, but several early Methodist writers offer clues. For example, Abel Stevens, a nineteenth-century Methodist historian, noted that many "charitably supposed that he [Allen] was insane." In his autobiography,

Trinity Episcopal Church sign, Highway 174, July 2013. *Terry Helsley, photographer.*

the Reverend Peter Cartwright compared Allen's downfall with that of King David because "in an evil hour [he] fell into sin"—that is, he "looked unlawfully on a young Lady and seduced her," suggesting that adultery was the cause of Allen's undoing. George Gilman Smith, another early Methodist historian, wrote that Allen committed a "flagrant crime" on Edisto Island. Regardless, the general consensus is that immorality— perhaps adultery—ended Allen's meteoric ministerial career.

FROM BAD TO WORSE

After leaving the ministry, Allen returned to Elbert County, Georgia, and there, with his brother William, operated a mercantile establishment near the Savannah River. Of interest, Allen also preached in the area. Unfortunately, all was not clear sailing; the enterprise did not flourish, and soon the brothers were in serious financial difficulties. On a buying trip to Augusta, they encountered a previous creditor. The creditor entered a complaint, and the United States marshal, Major Robert Forsyth, attempted to serve Allen with court papers in a civil suit. Forsyth was a Revolutionary War veteran and Georgia's first United States marshal.

On January 11, 1794, Forsyth and two deputies entered Mrs. Dixon's boardinghouse on Bay Street in Augusta looking for the Allen brothers. As an aside, Georgian historian Ed Cashin contends that another famous visitor, President George Washington, also stayed in Dixon's public house during his 1791 visit. As the brothers were in conversation and Forsyth did not want to interrupt, he requested a private word with Beverly and William Allen. Instead of cooperating with the lawman, they fled to an upstairs room and bolted the door behind them. Once inside, Allen cocked his loaded pistol and fired as he heard steps outside the door. The bullet passed through the wooden door and struck the forty-year-old Forsyth in the head. The unfortunate Forsyth died immediately and, as a result, became the first U.S. marshal to die in the line of duty.

Forsyth's deputies promptly arrested and incarcerated Beverly and William Allen. But before they could be tried, the Allen brothers escaped jail (possibly by bribing a jailer) and fled Augusta. At this point, this once prominent Methodist minister was guilty of murder and probably adultery.

Fleeing the authorities, Beverly and William Allen returned to Elbert County, where authorities promptly threw the Allen brothers into prison. While frontier sentiment often favored debtors, murder was quite a different story. Fortunately for Allen (if not justice), two hundred friends and relatives in the community, perhaps believing him mentally unstable, freed him from jail, after which Beverly Allen fled to the unsettled Kentucky frontier. His brother William remained undisturbed in Georgia.

FRONTIER EXILE

Allen's wife and family joined him in Kentucky. By 1804, Allen had settled in the Green River Valley of Logan County in a community appropriately known as Rogues' Harbor. In Order Book 2 for Logan County, transcribed by Judy Utley Lyne, there is an entry about Allen and his life there. Apparently, his proposal to build a dam for his sawmill on the main branch of the Red River aroused concerns among his neighbors. The sheriff summoned a jury to investigate the matter. After reviewing the evidence, the jury found that the dam would not flood offices, homes, gardens or orchards. The jury also ruled that the proposed retaining pond was not a health risk. Nevertheless, the jury limited the dam's height to six feet.

In Logan County, Allen farmed a one-thousand-acre tract near Russellville on the Red River, practiced medicine and adopted Universalism—apostasy for a Methodist. In his new home, despite his past, Allen was respected for his education and abilities and even tutored a future Methodist minister, Paul Cartwright. Cartwright's autobiography offers a personal perspective on the complicated character of Allen. In 1816, the apostate Beverly Allen died in Dot, Kentucky; he is buried in the Allen Family Cemetery there. The Reverend Peter Cartwright, a former student, visited the dying Allen, and according to Cartwright, Allen died believing his sins—though unspecified—were too great for God to forgive. Regrettably, even on his deathbed, Allen offered no insight into that fateful time on beautiful Edisto Island.

According to his will, Beverly and Anna Singletary Allen had nine children: Ann, Coke, Mary, Sarah, Martha, Carolina, Harriett, Hayes and William. After Beverly's death, Anna Allen continued to live in Logan County. In 1820, she lived in Russellville and headed a household that included eight white persons and thirty slaves. Ten years later, Anna Allen's household had shrunk to ten persons—four white and six enslaved. By 1850, Anna Allen no longer lived independently. Rather, the eighty-year-old widow was enumerated in the household of John and Nancy Crumbaugh.

In one more ironic twist, in 1799, the Second Great Awakening began in the Red River Presbyterian Church near Adairville in Logan County, Kentucky. This religious revival transformed the formerly lawless regions of Kentucky, spread across the eastern United States and triggered great growth for Christian denominations, especially the Methodist, Presbyterian and Baptist. Yet for some, Allen's apostasy negatively impacted the growth of Methodism in the South for decades.

However, the Allen influence in Georgia persisted. His brother William remained in Elbert County and prospered. Both of William's sons served in the Georgia legislature. Later, a lawyer named Young L.G. Harris married William's granddaughter Susan. Harris entered politics and was a critical player in the early history of Georgia as a judge and philanthropist. The names of the college and the city of Young Harris, Georgia, honor the life and work of this extraordinary man—a very different legacy than that of his great-uncle Beverly Allen.

Slings and Arrows

The Reverend Allen was not the only Edisto Island divine to face personal challenges. But the Reverend Mr. Donald A. McLeod was a different man with a different story. McLeod, a native of Glenelg Parish, Inverness-shire, Scotland, was a Presbyterian minister educated, according to his will, at King's College, Aberdeen, Scotland.

Possibly as early as 1710, Presbyterians were worshipping together on Edisto Island. In 1717, an island resident donated land to be placed in trust in order to support a Presbyterian minister on the island. Island residents and their church suffered during the Revolutionary years. A major postwar challenge was identifying and calling a desirable minister. For example, in 1790, according to Dudley Jones, the church voted against renewing the tenure of the current minister. Nevertheless, the next minister called refused to honor his contract with the church. So, on April 1, 1793, the church, mindful of past issues, invited McLeod to preach on a trial basis for six months. McLeod's salary was sixty pounds, with an additional twenty pounds allocated for his board.

On December 2, 1793, at the end of McLeod's trial period, the church called him full time. Apparently, the "polished and graceful" McLeod excelled and pleased the congregation despite his broad Scottish accent. One of McLeod's early successes was resolving a lengthy—and modern-sounding—dispute concerning seating in the church. The members voted to replace the box seats with pews. During his early years on Edisto, in 1795, McLeod married Elizabeth Bailey Seabrook. Elizabeth McLeod

Presbyterian Church on Edisto Island, July 2013. Reverend Donald McLeod served as pastor until his death in 1821. *Terry Helsley, photographer.*

was the daughter of James L. Clark and Mary Seabrook. The Reverend McLeod was her third husband. At age thirty-four, she died on October 18, 1802, on Edisto Island. Elizabeth Bailey Clark McLeod is buried in the Clark Burial Ground at Cypress Trees Plantation on Edisto Island. Her tombstone notes her "amiable & estimable qualities" and that "she lived respected & loved & died much lamented." The cemetery also includes the graves of two McLeod daughters: Mary, who died in 1810, and Mary Seabrook, who died in 1798.

AN UNEXPECTED, UNEXPLAINED BLIP

Surprisingly, given his success, in December 1803, McLeod resigned his position. Making his resignation even more mysterious, a year later, the church reissued its call to McLeod at a substantially higher salary. McLeod accepted the call and returned to his church responsibilities.

From available sources, it appears that the minister was the victim of personal and perhaps physical attacks—possibly from a disgruntled island resident. As described in *A Brief History of the Presbyterian Church of Edisto Island*, William Seabrook moved that the congregation appoint a committee "to retain counsel" who would work with the "public prosecutor" to bring to justice "the perpetrator" of a violent attack on the Reverend McLeod. In addition, the congregation requested the committee members to defend the minister's good name and "to repel the attempts which we believe are made to affect his character and to destroy his usefulness." Ephraim Mikell Sr. seconded the motion. The motion passed, and the church appointed Isaac Auld, James Clark and William Seabrook to serve on the committee.

Lacking specifics, Edisto historian Charles Spencer found the timing of the event significant. According to Spencer, McLeod's resignation occurred "less than six months after his second wife died." Therefore, the attack could involve "a misunderstanding about his relations with a woman."

From the wording of the motion, it appears not only that someone had attacked the minister but also that concurrently, someone had launched a concerted campaign to destroy his reputation as a minister. Whatever the specifics, the effort failed, and after his return, McLeod served as minister to the Edisto church until his death.

Nevertheless, McLeod's legal difficulties were not over. In February 1812, the Bank of South Carolina sued the minister for "certain promises…not performed" and damages. McLeod and J.J. Murray had signed a promissory note involving funds ($13,460) held by the executors of John Hanahan. Hanahan's executors were William Seabrook, James Clark, John Mikell and William Meggett, several of whom had been involved with McLeod's earlier difficulties. The Charleston District Court of Common Pleas heard the case and, in 1815, decided in favor of the bank. Nevertheless, it was February 1825 before Dr. J.B. Whitridge and his wife—the former Sarah Bailey McLeod, executrix of Reverend McLeod—finally settled the long-standing debt.

In 1812, Governor Henry Middleton proclaimed March 11 as a day "for Religious Reflection, Humiliation and Prayer." Consequently, on that date Reverend McLeod preached a sermon reflecting that theme. McLeod noted the "physical condition" of the country, acknowledged the "revolutionary vicissitudes" of the times and stressed the value of "life, liberty, and property—religion, security and self government." Later in 1812, McLeod published his erudite and well-argued sermon, dedicating it to the elders and trustees of the Presbyterian Church on Edisto Island.

On January 30, 1821, the Reverend Donald McLeod died of dropsy at Cypress Trees Plantation on Edisto Island. At his death, McLeod left one child, a daughter, Sarah Bailey McLeod. In his will, in addition to bequests to his daughter, he also bequeathed legacies to his five sisters in Scotland; his two sisters near Montreal, Canada; and a brother John in Glasgow, Scotland. McLeod also included funds for his former parish in Scotland. His daughter Sarah was his residual heir, as McLeod left his Wadmalaw plantation and personal property, including slaves, in trust for her. McLeod's executors were his daughter, William Seabrook Sr., Charles Gabriel Capers and William Edings. After his death, Sarah McLeod and Charles Gabriel Capers qualified as executors of his estate.

McLeod is buried in the Unitarian Church cemetery in Charleston. His epitaph notes, "Few men have descended to the tomb more regretted by an extensive circle or acquaintance than this learned and accomplished Divine." In honor of their beloved minister, the congregation on Edisto Island erected a marble monument in the church sanctuary.

ANOTHER CONTROVERSY

In the early twentieth century, members of the Presbyterian Church on Edisto were involved in a different controversy. The core of the controversy was the leadership of ruling elder Townsend Mikell. In 1917, the session and congregation took the unusual step of dissolving Mikell's official relationship with the church. Mikell protested the session's proceedings and, on October 16, 1917, appealed the decision to the Charleston Presbytery. The Reverend Dr. Melton Clark represented Mikell before the presbytery. Mikell's statement alleged that the church's actions were "hasty & devoid of reasonable indulgence." He also raised a number of procedural issues. Nevertheless, the presbytery, by a close vote, upheld the action of the Presbyterian Church on Edisto Island.

Apparently, some members of the congregation asserted that, despite efforts at negotiation, Mikell refused "to cooperate with the rest of the Church

Left: Session house, Presbyterian Church on Edisto Island, July 2013. *Terry Helsley, photographer.*

Below: Presbyterian Church on Edisto Island sign, July 2013. *Terry Helsley, photographer.*

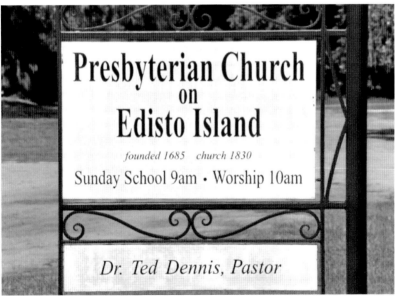

except on his *own arbitrary conditions*." Support for the current preacher, the Reverend S.C. Caldwell, was the tipping point in the relationship between Mikell and the church. Mikell was a ruling elder—a highly respected position of leadership in a Presbyterian church. In this period, elders were generally professionals and successful businessmen. Challenging one was a serious undertaking. The session was the governing body of the local church.

Mikell apparently threw down the proverbial gauntlet when he refused to contribute to the preacher's salary. As Mikell wrote, "I consider that his stay among us is a detriment to the life of the Church." Mikell, in his defense, was willing, when the present minister left, to contribute to the support of his successor. Yet according to one source, the church unanimously—that is, "with no dissenting votes save from those bound by family obligations"— voted that Mikell was "unacceptable" as elder.

Although Mikell lost his official position with the Presbyterian Church on Edisto Island, his letter of June 17, 1917, seized the high ground. It was addressed to the Reverend S.C. Caldwell and elders William Murray, William Edings and T.C. Murray. Mikell eloquently cited his seventy-six years of membership and his lifetime of service and support for the "physical, moral and spiritual life of the church." He also alluded to an "outside influence" that currently disrupted the "welfare" of the church. Mikell said he was surprised by the congregation's action yet felt at peace. The Lord, according to Mikell, was "telling me that my work for him on earth is nearly ended." After receipt of Mikell's letter, on July 1, 1917, William Murray, clerk of the session, wrote Mikell ending Mikell's "official relation with the Presbyterian Church of Edisto Island."

According to a history of the church, Mikell and the Reverend S.C. Caldwell were not always at odds. In April 1911, the church held a ceremony commemorating the first year of the church's third century. As part of the celebration, Caldwell presented the pre–Civil War history of the church, and Townsend Mikell then shared the postwar history. Caldwell was pastor of the Presbyterian Church on Edisto Island from 1906 until 1918. Townsend Mikell, planter and civil leader, died on Edisto Island in 1926.

Watchful Waiting

Independence was not easy for the new United States. Despite the peace treaty that ended the American Revolution, major issues still festered between the new country and Great Britain. Among these issues were the continued presence of British military forces on American soil and American access to markets in the Caribbean. Lack of progress with negotiations and resentment of perceived British patronization eventually led to war. A group of representatives in the United States Congress known as the "War Hawks" advocated war. Among these were two South Carolinians: Andrew Jackson (then living in Tennessee) and John C. Calhoun. The war party prevailed, and the United States and Great Britain squared off for round two: the War of 1812. On June 18, 1812, the United States Congress declared war on Great Britain.

DEFENDING THE COAST

Unfortunately, due to President Thomas Jefferson's drastic military cuts, the United States was ill prepared for war. Britain was a major sea and land power, but fortunately for the United States, it was occupied with defeating Napoleon Bonaparte. So it was 1814 before the British could focus all their attention on the American conflict. Nevertheless, the British did establish a naval blockade of the Atlantic coast and attempt to harass American shipping.

Paul Hamilton house, Edisto Island, 1938. Paul Hamilton (1761–1816) served as secretary of the navy under President James Madison. His great-grandfather John Hamilton married Mary Grimball, daughter of Paul Grimball. *Frances Benjamin Johnston, photographer. Library of Congress, Prints and Photographs Division, LC-DIG-csas-03736.*

In November 1812, with the war effort progressing slowly, President James Madison named a new secretary of the navy and a new secretary of war. Although naval successes were the only bright spots in the early months of the war, Madison asked Paul Hamilton to resign for health issues and, in his place, appointed William Jones. As a result, Jones, a merchant, banker and sea captain, replaced Hamilton, a man with family connections to the South Carolina Lowcountry and Edisto Island. Jones had served on a Pennsylvania privateer during the American Revolution and in the United States House of Representatives.

Facing again the prospects of invasion, South Carolina—especially the Lowcountry, with its many bays, creeks and rivers—was justifiably concerned. The region had seen incursions from Yemassee, Spaniards, pirates and, during the American Revolution, the English. The post-Revolutionary years brought new challenges.

QUASI-WAR WITH FRANCE

Privateers were not new to Edisto. For example, in 1798, the *Greenfield Gazette* (Massachusetts) reported that three privateers had visited Edisto Island. This incursion during the Quasi-War with France heightened uncertainties along the eastern seaboard. The Quasi-War was an undeclared war between the United States and the French Republic that lasted from 1798 to 1800. This war was fought primarily at sea until the Convention of 1800 (Treaty of Mortefontaine) restored relations between the two former allies.

The Quasi-War was the American response to the XYZ Affair. In 1796, French authorities had issued an order permitting French vessels (privateers) to seize American merchant ships. In an effort to eliminate this threat, President John Adams sent three envoys—Elbridge Gerry, Charles Cotesworth Pinckney (of South Carolina) and John Marshall—to negotiate with the French. When the Americans arrived, they intended to meet with the French foreign minister, the Marquis de Talleyrand. Instead, three French agents approached the Americans and demanded certain concessions and a large bribe before the Americans could see Talleyrand. At this point, Pinckney uttered the famous phrase, "No, no, not a sixpence." When news of this insult reached the United States Congress, many wanted to declare war on France. Adams opposed war, and while he negotiated a diplomatic solution, the undeclared war continued to impact American shipping, ports and exposed coastal areas.

In 1798, sixteen armed men from the three privateers landed on Edisto. The men seized sheep and poultry, for which they paid six dollars, and attempted to collect intelligence about the inhabitants. In particular, they asked about the numbers of black and white residents and the wealth of Edisto planters. As a result, "great terror and alarm" filled the South Carolina Lowcountry.

SOUTH CAROLINA LOWCOUNTRY IN THE WAR OF 1812

J.H. Dent was the naval officer in charge of protecting South Carolina. Stationed in Charleston, Dent repeatedly sparred with the secretary of the navy, William Jones, over the management of operations in South Carolina and the size of the naval contingent deployed for the state's protection.

At the beginning of 1813, Dent had barges and four schooners—*Alligator, Carolina, Ferret* and *Nonsuch*—to protect the South Carolina coast. In February

1813, Dent reported on construction at the Charleston Navy Yard, his efforts to secure appropriate space for a hospital and British efforts to disrupt the inland trade by capturing coasting vessels in Bull's Bay. He also bemoaned the lack of available sailors to man his ships. As he noted, "What few men are here, are either taken by the privateers, or engaged for France, at 45 dollars per month."

On May 8, 1813, Dent reported to Jones that the British had one sloop and two brigs blockading Charleston Harbor. In addition, there was a British privateer, *Dash*, raiding coasting vessels and capturing their cargo and crews. The British also "made some captures inland." With South Carolina's exposed rivers and bays, it was difficult to protect South Carolina inland shipping and settlements from privateers.

As a result of Dent's reports of the dire situation in the Lowcountry and the many petitions from the inhabitants of Charleston, Secretary Jones reversed an earlier order (dated February 28) removing the South Carolina gunboats from active duty. On May 27, he ordered additional barges to "protect merchant vessels against the small British cruisers." Dent then had more vessels than he had crew to man. Jones also rebuffed Dent's efforts to improve the navy yard in Charleston, improve medical facilities and establish an outpost at Beaufort. The frustrated Dent repeatedly requested his own ship or to be allowed to return to Washington.

THE EDISTO EXPERIENCE

Edisto Island, framed by the South Edisto and North Edisto Rivers, did not escape the challenges of this new war with Britain. According to Whitson Brooks, in 1971 while surveying the golf course, David Lybrand found an old fort. Lybrand and his brother determined that the structure dated from the War of 1812. Troops were stationed on the island and probably at the fort. But as the British did not invade South Carolina, such coastal fortifications saw no action. Reportedly, after South Carolina seceded, General P.G.T. Beauregard surveyed the facility but found little of interest. According to Clara Puckette, the Lybrands also found two cannons on the southern part of the beach: one in 1959 and the other in 1974 at the site of the Oristo development. The two cannons dated from the Revolutionary era. One of them, dated 1765, now stands beside Edisto Realty on Palmetto Boulevard.

The golf course with sedge and lagoon, Wyndham Resort, December 2013. Reportedly, in the 1970s during construction of the golf course, Dave Lybrand found the ruins of a War of 1812 fort. *Terry Helsley, photographer.*

Although the fort (or forts) saw no action during the War of 1812, the residents of Edisto did. In February 1814, the presence of a British frigate off Edisto Island excited alarm. Residents feared the enemy would land at any time. In late January 1815, according to the *Virginia Patriot*, British forces landed on Edisto Island, "spiked the guns of a small battery, and burnt the dwelling-houses of Wm. Seabrook and Benj. Bailey, Esq'rs. Which were situated near the battery." In addition, there was firing between American and British ships offshore. Major B. Robertson, the John's Island commander, also reported alarms at the Edisto Island fort, on Wadmalaw and on John's Island.

Another report stated that Major Robertson sent a detachment from his John's Island battalion to Edisto. These fifty men joined twenty militiamen from Edisto and captured seventy marauders who were on the island "sinking wells and killing cattle." The interest in wells and cattle suggests that the marauders were from a naval vessel in need of fresh water and food. A later report of L. Kearney on the naval action off the island supports this conclusion. According to his statement, on January 29, he learned that a watering party from a British warship was on Edisto Island. Kearney and his barge attempted to intercept three vessels rowing toward the British ship. Two escaped, but Kearney and his crew captured a tender with "one long 9 pounder" cannon aboard. One of Kearney's crew died during the firefight.

Blood on the Sand

Dueling was a way of life for antebellum gentlemen. Death was considered preferable to dishonor. There were protocols governing the exercise and rules that the participants had to follow. According to I. Jenkins Mikell, the dueling site on antebellum Edisto Island was the "sands," a strip of beach within earshot of the surf near Edingsville.

EDINGSVILLE

Edingsville was a resort on the beach where planters and their families normally retired each May to avoid the sickly summer months. One resident described the area as a "long and narrow sand hill." Households packed up furnishings and supplies. Family and friends relocated en masse. The women and young enjoyed the social life, and the men were close enough to their plantations to visit occasionally. Slave workers brought fresh vegetables and meat from the home plantations to supplement the abundant seafood and kitchen gardens. The village of Edingsville had two rows of houses, a store and a church.

During the Civil War, New Englanders occasionally visited the desolate resort. For example, in 1864, Charlotte Forten left St. Helena Island for an excursion to Edingsville. Two rowboats carried the party to its destination. As they were traveling through enemy territory, the boat crews and accompanying officer were armed with "guns and cutlasses." To Forten, the houses had a

Tree-lined stretch of Edingsville Beach Road, Edisto Island, July 2013. On May 11, 1865, Mary Ann Ames described a similar stretch of road: "The road shaded and cool, winding under live-oak trees covered with moss, the wild grape was in bloom and the air filled with the perfume." *Terry Helsley, photographer.*

"desolate, dismantled look," yet she enjoyed collecting "beautiful tiny shells which were buried deep in the sand." The party spent the night in several of the abandoned houses and took a moonlit walk on the beach listening to the roar of the waves. To Forten, the moonlight made the empty houses and uncultivated gardens appear "still wilder and more desolate." By 1865, the island was still unoccupied, and Mary Ann Ames, a Freedmen's Bureau teacher from Massachusetts, crossed on a raft to Edingsville and "walked to the long row of houses on the beach." Despite the planters' abandoning the island when war broke out, Ames found several of the houses "very pretty." She admired the broad stretch of sand and found the surf "grand."

Yet life at Edingsville was not always enjoyable—at least in the post–Civil War years. For example, in 1870, Selina McCarthy Graham wrote a friend from Edingsville. Graham noted her disgust with the climate and "maroon life." Maroons were runaway slaves who established temporary communities on the fringes of settled areas. She found the society "disgusting" yet noted that the Townsend family had a "happy faculty for entertaining pleasantly." Graham continued to assert that the jokes about Edisto residents were true. Nevertheless, she noted that on "bright days the view is magnificent."

Rock groin, Edisto Beach, December 2012. *Jacob Helsley, photographer.*

Bailey store, Highway 174, July 2013. This building is one of the few surviving Edingsville structures. It was dismantled and moved here from the resort settlement. *Terry Helsley, photographer.*

In 1854, the quiet village Edingsville also had a suspicious death. On May 3, coroner J.P. Deveaux convened an inquest into the death of Timothy Clancy. Clancy, possibly a native of Ireland, worked at the saltworks at Edingsville on Edisto Island. In the antebellum period (and later), workers produced salt through the evaporation of salt water in shallow pools or ponds. The coroner's jury viewed Clancy's "horribly mangled" body and interviewed witnesses. From the evidence, it concluded that the killer hit Clancy "with an axe on the right side of the front part of the head." Furthermore, the jury averred that Clancy died as a consequence of the blows. Apparently, Clancy died at the home of his friend Henry Smith in Edingsville. Although no motive was uncovered, based on the evidence, authorities arrested Smith for the crime. Smith protested his innocence, and the outcome of this case is uncertain.

Due to its location on a barrier island, Edingsville was always under assault from the elements. For example, a planter wrote from Edisto in 1837 that hurricane winds and tides had "ripped away" twenty feet of the beachfront. In August 1881, the *Charleston News & Courier* reported, "The existence of Edingsville village has now ended." Though diminished, the village persevered until the Hurricane of 1893 pounded the island for fourteen hours and washed away the remnants of the once-beloved summer resort. As Henry A.M. Smith noted in 1918, "The site of the village of Edingsville on the Ocean edge of Edisto Island" has been "entirely swept away and is now in the ocean."

Duels

Sometimes, these affairs of honor ended peacefully. For example, I. Jenkins Mikell wrote of a duel fought because one man, following a domestic dispute, granted "sanctuary" to another man's wife. In this instance, although shots were fired, no one was injured, and the seconds eventually negotiated a nonviolent resolution. On another occasion, a man remarked on a woman's bathing attire. Another man was offended and demanded a retraction and apology. The first man refused, and the other man challenged him to a duel. Surprisingly, he refused to defend his honor and declined the duel. As a result, a family member accepted the challenge to defend the family honor. The two met at the sands. Both fired, but neither was hit. In the end, the seconds declared the matter settled. So, at times, seconds or other friends could intervene and mediate conflicts. But at other times, hotter heads prevailed, and the principals with their seconds repaired to the sands.

GILLON V. WILSON

One such instance was the Gillon-Wilson affair. On July 11, 1832, John Wilson killed Alexander Gillon in a duel fought at "Eddings [*sic*] Bay, Edisto Island." The reason for the duel is unknown. The victim was the thirty-seven-year-old son of Commodore Alexander Gillon and his second wife, Ann Purcell. Commodore Gillon was a colorful Charleston Patriot. Reputedly born in Rotterdam, Gillon served as captain of the German Fusiliers, and in 1778, the new state of South Carolina named him commodore of the South Carolina navy. Later, the senior Gillon also represented South Carolina in the United States House of Representatives. In addition to other property, Gillon owned a plantation on the Congaree River called Gillon's Retreat. Commodore Gillon died in 1795.

On December 17, 1816, at St. Michael's Church in Charleston, the younger Gillon married Sarah Harriet Brisbane. Sarah (b. 1797) was the daughter of John Stanyarne Brisbane, who owned Malona on the Ashley River. Her grandfather James Stanyarne was a Loyalist who was banished from Charleston in 1782. Sarah Brisbane Gillon died in 1828, several years before the death of her husband. According to the Gillon family Bible, Alexander Gillon, the duel victim, was buried on Edisto Island.

GILLING V. BAILEY

In such cases, dueling was a deadly exercise. One of the often-told dueling stories on Edisto Island concerns Arthur Alfred Gilling and an unidentified Edisto resident named Bailey. Jenkins Mikell recounts the story of the young Englishman Gilling and the Edisto native Bailey, the former considered an expert shot and the latter extraordinarily inept with pistols. Neither the nature of the dispute nor Bailey's first name survives the years—an interesting oversight. Nevertheless, as with fish, over time embellishments appeared. For example, according to a reporter for a Charleston newspaper, Gilling was an arrogant Englishman visiting in Charleston. When he heard of the quiet backwater of Edisto and its unsophisticated residents, he decided, as a lark, to visit the island. On Edisto, his high-handed ways led to the dispute that cost Gilling his life, as the allegedly superior marksman fell victim to the man who could not hit the proverbial "barn door." The mattress Bailey had reputedly brought to convey his own body home instead carried Gilling to his final resting place.

Presbyterian Church on Edisto Island, 1940. The churchyard is the final resting place for Arthur A. Gilling. *C.O. Greene, photographer. Courtesy of Library of Congress, Prints & Photographs Division, HABS SC,10-EDIL,3-1.*

The surviving records reveal little about the marksmanship of the opponents or the nature of the confrontation. Even Gilling's grave in the historic Presbyterian churchyard sheds little light on those fateful moments. The inscription on his tombstone reads:

> *In Memory*
> *Of*
> *Arthur Alfred Gilling*
> *A native of London England*
> *Born 19th of June 1811*
> *And died 12th Feb. 1839*
> *Prepare to meet thy God.*

Only the final line of the inscription suggests the unpredictability of life and perhaps hints at the unexpected death of the young man.

Tombstone of Arthur Alfred Gilling, Presbyterian Church on Edisto Island, January 2014. Gilling was a young merchant killed in a duel at Edingsville. *Terry Helsley, photographer.*

Yet Gilling was not an idle, arrogant interloper whose chance encounter with the men of Edisto led to his death on the sands of Edingsville. Rather, Gilling was a businessman, merchant, husband and father. Although a native of England, Gilling had been in the state for several years and had business connections with Edisto Island.

As early as June 1835, Arthur Alfred Gilling, a native of London, England, was living in Charleston, as a local newspaper announced he had mail. On May 5, 1838, according to an advertisement in the *Southern Patriot*, Charles Miller and Arthur A. Gilling of Edisto Island announced that on October 1, 1837, the subscribers had formed a business connection. Gilling actively pursued his vocation, and according to shipping notices, on May 23, 1838, he traveled, probably on business, from Savannah to Beaufort. Even after his untimely death, on January 13, 1840, a Charleston newspaper announced the arrival of merchandise that Gilling had ordered from Bankman, New York, for his store on Edisto Island.

Gilling's Marriage

On April 4, 1838, the Reverend Mr. Adam Gilchrist married Mrs. Mary J. Nohr, née Monefeldt, to Arthur Alfred Gilling in Walterboro, South Carolina. Mrs. Gilling's first husband may have been Thor Todberg Nohr, who died in 1830 at age thirty-three and is buried in Magnolia Cemetery in Charleston. The Gillings' wedded bliss was short, as only a year and a few months later, Mary Gilling, either pregnant or the recent mother of a baby daughter (also named Mary), learned that her second young husband was dead. She never remarried.

From available records, it appears that in order to support her family, Mary Gilling returned to her teaching roots. According to the 1830–31 *Charleston City Directory*, Mrs. and Miss Monefeldt operated a school for "young ladies" on Beaufain Street in Charleston. In 1840, Mrs. Mary Gilling lived in St. Bartholomew Parish, Colleton District, South Carolina. Her household included four individuals: two female adults and two children, a boy and a girl. She operated a school, probably in Walterboro, and according to the census, she had twenty-two students.

By 1850, Mary Gilling, age forty, was still a teacher and operated a school in St. Bartholomew's Parish. Her multigenerational household included her daughter, Mary Catherine Gilling (age eleven); her mother, Marie H. Monefeldt (age sixty-five and a native of Denmark); her sister Julia A. Davenport (age forty-two); and Davenport's son Charles A. Davenport (age four and born in Massachusetts). Her household also included one slave, perhaps Philip, whom Mary Gilling purchased from Ansley Davis in February 1841. According to the *Charleston Observer*, on February 12, 1844, Julia A. Monefeldt had married William Ward Davenport.

Mary Gilling's mother, Marie Hedevic Monefeldt, née Schottman, a native of Copenhagen, Denmark, died on February 7, 1860. By Monefeldt's will, Mary J. Gilling, her daughter, was the primary legatee. Monefeldt left Gilling her silver, household furnishings, clothing and stock of wine. Monefeldt also left legacies for her grandchildren: Mary C. Gilling (daughter of Mary and Arthur A. Gilling), Justina Howland, Ilione Howland, Sarah M. Howland, Laura D. Howland, William Monefeldt Howland and Charles Augusts Davenport (son of Julia and William Ward Davenport).

On September 16, 1880, the long-widowed Mary Johnston Nohr Gilling died. Born on October 10, 1808, the eighty-one-year-old Gilling succumbed to breast cancer in New Orleans. Having spent the last twenty years of her life in Charleston, her body was shipped back to Charleston and buried in Magnolia Cemetery. In addition to birth and death dates, Mary Gilling's grave marker states, "Widow of Arthur Alfred Gilling." While her mother and other family members are also buried there, the husband she mourned is buried miles away in an Edisto churchyard.

Gilling's Business Partner

According to the *Charleston City Directory* of 1830–31, Gilling's partner, Charles E. Miller, was a merchant operating a business from Chisolm's wharf in Charleston. At that time, Miller lived at 52 Anson Street in Charleston. Later, Miller built and operated a store on Edisto Island. In 1835, Miller purchased from John Hanahan three acres on the eastern side of the public road on Edisto Island, the site of his store. Miller's store apparently stood near the site of Bailey's store because when William and Martha Whaley conveyed "Valentine's lot" (an acre) on the eastern side of the public road on Edisto Island to Henry F. Bailey, the description of the property notes that the lot adjoined "land known lately as Miller's Lot and Store."

Unfortunately, Miller's mercantile activities on Edisto did not survive the death of his partner and may have been a factor in Gilling's duel. On November 2, 1839, Miller, citing "losses in trade, and the severe pressure of the times," conveyed his stock in trade, bills due and land on Edisto Island to William A. Caldwell of Charleston in trust for Miller's creditors. Several of Miller's creditors, such as Edward Whaley and the Bank of South Carolina, had previously obtained judgments against Miller. But Miller had other creditors, and his indebtedness exceeded $38,000. Nevertheless, Miller listed his primary obligation as a $5,000 bond he owed Mrs. M.J. Nohr Gilling, widow of his late partner. In addition to Whaley, who had invested in Miller's enterprise, Miller also owed money to J.M McLeod of Edisto. Miller's creditors included merchants and firms not only in Charleston but also in New York, Boston and Kingston, Rhode Island. Miller's assets included a carriage and pair of carriage horses, a sorrel horse, a barouche, a gig, a sulky, tack and household and kitchen furniture valued at less than $3,000. Miller also owned a tract of three hundred acres that "derived from John Hanahan from Joseph S. Murray." The tract fronted on the public road and included "that portion of land on which the said Charles Miller has lately erected his store dwelling, house and outbuildings." Under the agreement, Caldwell took control of Miller's assets in trust for his creditors. Later in 1839, Caldwell conveyed the lot with the store on Edisto Island to Alexander Calder. This rapid turnover suggests the great interest in the Miller store location.

Edisto Island, Charleston District, *Mills Atlas of South Carolina*, 1825. The Mills map shows a store on the public road near Store Creek. *Collection of the author.*

This Calder may be related to the William Calder who in 1839 entered into partnership with George H. Milnor to operate a "country store" on Edisto Island. By 1852, this partnership had dissolved; the men continued in business until at least 1858 but not without controversy. The partnership was dissolved; Milnor claimed insolvency, and their clerk, bookkeeper and brother-in-law, Samuel F. Corrie, sued Calder for funds due him. Calder objected to

Old Post Office Restaurant, July 2013. For years, Bailey's Store and the post office were centers of island life. *Terry Helsley, photographer.*

Store Creek, Edisto Island, July 2013. *Terry Helsley, photographer.*

Milnor testifying on behalf of Corrie, and in 1853, the case reached the South Carolina Court of Appeals, which upheld the verdict on Corrie's behalf.

As part of the conveyance to Caldwell, Miller also listed his stock in trade that remained in his store on Edisto Island and debts owed. Miller's creditors included residents of Charleston, Wadmalaw and Edisto. From the list of Edisto creditors, the Miller-Gilling establishment was popular with island residents. Among the creditors were Henry Swinton, Joseph B. Seabrook, Joseph E. Jenkins, William M. Murray, A.J. Clark, William G. Baynard, Emma E. Seabrook, B.L. Edings, James C. Meggett, William States Lee (pastor of the Presbyterian Church), Captain Daniel Townsend, Dr. William M. Bailey and Edward D. Bailey.

So while the cause of the duel in February 1839 remains a mystery, the backgrounds of Gilling and his partner, Miller, suggest several possibilities: business conflicts or competition on the island or even a dispute over the amount or repayment of a debt. Regardless, one of the protagonists chose a drastic method to defend his personal honor.

Despite the plantation lifestyle, residents on Edisto Island wanted goods and services that even the most self-sufficient plantation could not offer. Consequently, as early as 1825, according to Mills Atlas, there was a store on Edisto Island on the public road near Store Creek. Goods arrived by water and overland.

As a result, merchants in Charleston, Walterboro and perhaps Beaufort and Savannah viewed Edisto Island as both a potential market and an opportunity for expansion. Both Gilling and Miller had connections with Charleston and Walterboro. Gilling married and lived in Walterboro, and in 1830, so did Charles Miller. Also, at one time, Miller and Gilling lived and worked in Charleston. To these young men, like many others, Edisto Island was a land of opportunity. But their dream was short-lived, ending in death for one and bankruptcy for the other. Yet the location continued to attract commercial operations.

Today, the store building on or near the site of Miller's failed experiment is known as Bailey's store. Is it ironic or coincidental that an unknown Bailey killed Gilling in 1839, leaving the twice-widowed Mary Johnston Gilling to support and rear their young daughter alone? The story continues to be told and retold, but more questions than answers remain. Questions such as: Why is the name of the victim preserved and not that of the shooter? What point of honor could draw a young husband with a newborn baby or a pregnant wife to risk his livelihood? What was the role of Gilling's demise in the failure of Miller's business on Edisto Island? Was there local resentment of the Miller and Gilling partnership or others who wanted to control the prime commercial location on the island? And was one of Miller's creditors the Bailey who shot Gilling on that fateful day?

Crime and Punishment

In 1823, Charleston residents were coping with the shock of the Vesey rebellion of 1822. Denmark Vesey was a free black who had purchased his freedom, a businessman and leader in the African Methodist Episcopal church in Charleston. Fortunately for Charleston, a few of the slaves approached about the conspiracy told their owners of the plot. One of the identified conspirators even belonged to the governor. Upon learning of the proposed insurrection, the authorities acted quickly. They arrested and then interrogated 131 accused conspirators. Based on testimony received, 67 of the accused were convicted, and 35 individuals, including Vesey, the organizer, were executed. Other slaves involved in the plot were banished from the state. White South Carolinians were uneasy and warily eyed their black workers with suspicion.

South Carolina Association

In the aftermath of the Vesey scare, some Charleston residents looked for ways to better control the city's large free and enslaved black populations. For some, law enforcement officials seemed prone to react to situations rather than to proactively prevent them. These residents wanted all legal restrictions on black residents—slave or free—vigorously enforced. In Charleston, some of these men organized the South Carolina Association,

Tabby foundation, cotton gin, Sunnyside plantation, Edisto Island. Cultivating sea-island cotton required a large slave workforce. *Courtesy of Library of Congress, Prints & Photographs Division, HABS SC,10-EDIL,8D-1.*

a vigilante group, to enforce the Negro laws and limit contact between city and country blacks. Despite its extralegal nature, the association was popular with residents, and other areas, including Edisto Island, applauded the idea and organized auxiliaries. On November 18, 1823, officers of the Edisto Island Auxiliary Association petitioned the South Carolina General Assembly for incorporation. The officers of the new society were William Seabrook, president; Benjamin Bailey and John R. Mathewes, vice-presidents; William Edings, treasurer; and Whitemarsh B. Seabrook, secretary.

In the petition, Seabrook and the others, motivated, as they noted, by a "sacred regard for the safety of their property," asked to form an auxiliary association of Edisto Island in order to aid the "constituted authorities with respect to the regulation of the Coloured [*sic*] Population." Citing the inability of the police to be everywhere at all times, the petitioners stated that despite the best efforts of the police, "the mid-night incendiary has escaped with impunity and the assassin perfected his schemes of horror."

In addition, the petitioners argued, the need on Edisto Island was more acute than elsewhere in the state. The petitioners cited population statistics to support their need: the "white population of Edisto Island is to the Black as 200 to 3000, or as 1 to 15." As Seabrook and company clearly stated, "[W]ith our mixed and peculiar population, it is vitally important, not only that the provisions of the Legislature relative to the government of our Slaves, should be strictly and rigidly enforced, but that no aberration from the line of policy, marked out by the State should ever be permitted."

In other words, planters on Edisto Island found the association a necessary tool to preserve order. Residents supported the association and its goal of enforcing the letter of the law and eliminating gray areas in black/white interaction. The South Carolina legislature granted the request, and the Edisto association set to work. The specificity of the references to an incendiary and assassin suggest an underlying reality to the Edisto planters' concerns. Nevertheless, it is not known how long the association functioned on Edisto Island. The parent association in Charleston renewed its charter in the late 1840s but ceased to function in the 1850s.

The Wandering *Wanderer*

Although the United States outlawed the international slave trade in 1808, the illegal smuggling and enslaving of Africans continued. The Sea Islands of South Carolina and Georgia were (and are) geographically suited for smuggling. Pirates and privateers frequented the coast. Place names such as Privateer Point commemorate the connection. The many Lowcountry waterways offer routes that avoid the more heavily traveled shore routes. The rivers and creeks link innumerable islands. There was no way federal agents could police the coast. The illegal trade continued. From Sam Gadsden's family history, it is clear that Dutch traders and others brought slaves into Wadmalaw and Edisto between 1808 and 1820.

As the law was being ignored, Congress acted to strengthen the legislation. On May 15, 1820, in an effort to eradicate this trade, the United States Congress enacted legislation "declaring certain acts by the master and crew of a vessel, relative to negroes, piracy." The legislation also gave federal courts—in the states where the offense was committed—jurisdiction in such cases. That proviso had unanticipated consequences. Accused South Carolina smugglers found a friendly venue in the federal district court in Charleston. Federal authorities also sent gunboats to patrol the coasts of Florida, Georgia and South Carolina. Consequently, U.S. naval vessels intercepted several ships with illegal slave cargos.

One of the more famous antebellum cases involved a specially built racing yacht named the *Wanderer*. Rigged as a schooner, the *Wanderer* was sleek and fast. In 1857, Thomas B. Hawkins built the yacht at the Joseph Rowland

The *Wanderer* was a sleek racing yacht built in New York. William C. Corrie of South Carolina purchased the yacht and refitted it as a slave ship. *From* Harper's Weekly Illustrated.

shipyard in Setauket on Long Island, New York. Colonel John Johnson of New York and Louisiana was the *Wanderer*'s original owner. On its maiden voyage, the captain sailed the yacht from Long Island down the Atlantic coast to New Orleans and then back to New York City. During the voyage, among other ports of call, the *Wanderer* docked at Charleston.

After the *Wanderer*'s return to New York, several southern investors eyed the fast vessel with great interest. As a result, William C. Corrie, a Lowcountry resident, with the assistance of Charles A.L. Lamar, of Charleston, purchased the yacht. Corrie and Lamar wanted to adapt the sleek yacht for use in the illegal slave trade. Lamar grew up in Savannah and was a "fire eater," meaning that he actively supported secession. Consequently, Lamar wanted to use the issue of the slave trade to divide the North and South. In pursuit of his goal, Lamar had earlier outfitted two other vessels for the Atlantic slave trade—the *Rawlins* and the *Richard Cobden*—without success. In July 1858, Lamar asked the Charleston collector of customs to clear the *Richard Cobden* for a trip to Havana to collect a "cargo of…'Asiatic Apprentices,'" but the collector denied Lamar's request. Undismayed, Lamar continued his efforts, and his collaboration with Corrie to acquire the *Wanderer* was his third attempt to import slaves illegally into the United States.

With Lamar's support, Corrie had the yacht modified. Some of Corrie's modifications raised eyebrows. For example, he had water tanks installed that could hold fifteen thousand gallons. The tanks and other modifications suggested to observers that Corrie was having the *Wanderer* outfitted as a slave vessel. Acting on these suspicions, a federal revenue cutter stopped the *Wanderer* as it tried to leave New York Harbor, and federal officials carefully inspected the vessel. While they found accoutrements appropriate for the slave trade, there was no "smoking gun"—nothing that conclusively linked the ship with the illegal trade.

Cleared for departure, the ship sailed south and on June 24, 1859, reached Charleston. From there, after additional adjustments, on July 3 the *Wanderer* sailed for Trinidad. From Trinidad, Corrie's ship departed on July 27 and sailed across the Atlantic Ocean. On September 16, the *Wanderer* entered the Congo River. After acquiring 500 Africans, Corrie and crew departed in October for the United States. He had hired several Portuguese sailors experienced in the slave trade to assist with the return journey. It was a difficult voyage, and many of the slave cargo died. Yet according to one source, the *Wanderer* arrived with 407 Africans for sale. Eventually, on November 27, the *Wanderer* reached Jekyll Island, Georgia, one of the "Golden Isles of Georgia."

On November 1, the *Charleston Mercury* ran a notice from the Washington correspondent of the *Baltimore American*. The notice suggested that federal officials working to prevent the illegal importation of slaves should investigate the *Wanderer* and its owner, William C. Corrie. At that time, the yacht with its captain and owner Corrie "was lying *perdu* [out of sight] at Edisto Island." Corrie lived, according to *The Rudder*, a magazine, on "a plantation on the North Edisto River, about 20 miles south of Charleston." In addition, the correspondent also identified a man named Trowbridge as essential to the nefarious project. Nelson C. Trowbridge, a native of Vermont, had lived in Georgia and was in 1859 a resident of New York. According to Trowbridge's "own frequent and open admissions," he was an investor in the *Wanderer* project and personally was on hand when the illegally imported Africans came ashore. Trowbridge then directed their dispersion.

Word of the illegal arrival of slave cargo spread quickly. According to the *Savannah Republican*, the Africans landed near Brunswick on Jekyll Island. Traders paid $15,000 to be involved and loaded 150 slaves of the estimated

300 imported on a steamboat and sailed them past Savannah to a plantation upriver. While several hundred of the Africans were sold near Brunswick, Georgia, others found their way to South Carolina, Mississippi, Alabama and other southern states. For example, an observer spotted 38 of the imported Africans in Montgomery, Alabama.

Although in 1859 authorities were unable to rescue the captive Africans, those involved in the operation faced civil and criminal prosecutions. Following the arrival of the *Wanderer*, federal agents arrested Captain William C. Corrie in South Carolina. Corrie made an almost triumphal entrance into Charleston. In the South, he was a hero. An announcement in the *Edgefield Advertiser* stated that Corrie and his associates acted "from purely patriotic motives." In Charleston, federal judge Andrew G. Magrath, a southern rights advocate, heard the Corrie case. Invoking a liberal interpretation of the 1820 statute, Magrath ruled that the evidence did not support a charge of smuggling and freed the captain. In the last months of the Civil War, Magrath was the last Confederate governor of South Carolina.

During a Fourth of July celebration in 1859, residents of nearby Walterboro voiced their support for Corrie and his activities. Celebrants there raised toasts to the reopened slave trade. Corrie's flaunting of federal law resonated with many southerners.

In 1859, officials also arrested John Dubignon, another resident of Savannah, for holding Africans as slaves and Nelson C. Trowbridge for importing and holding slaves. In Augusta, officials arrested the *Wanderer*'s crew. Despite Lamar's efforts to bribe witnesses and organize a jailbreak, the men were tried and convicted. Authorities indicted Lamar and declared the *Wanderer* forfeit. But in a strange twist, by April, Lamar was free and allowed to repurchase his ship for $4,001. Having learned little from his experience, Lamar refitted the vessel and attempted another slave-raiding voyage. Again, officials seized the *Wanderer* and declared it forfeit. Yet Lamar appeared in court and once more regained the ship.

According to Tom Henderson Wells, Trowbridge was the agent who supervised the outfitting of the *Wanderer*. He had also had other dealings with Charles Lamar, and during the Civil War, he was the New York agent who represented Lamar's blockade-running enterprises.

With the outbreak of the Civil War, the *Wanderer*'s slave-trading days ended. Federal naval forces captured the schooner in Key West and refitted it as a blockade ship. Ironically, the *Wanderer* then successfully intercepted a number of Southern blockade runners.

Steamboat Landing, Edisto Island, July 2013. Steamboat Creek flows into the North Edisto River. *Terry Helsley, photographer.*

On December 26, 1870, William C. Corrie, a prime mover in this dark tale and a resident of the Mills House, died in Charleston from Bright's disease (acute or chronic nephritis). He is buried in Magnolia Cemetery.

The last word, unexpectedly, belongs to the unwilling illegal immigrants. Emancipation ended their servitude. A 1908 article in the *American Anthropologist* detailed information about a few of these individuals. Several of the individuals interviewed by Charles J. Montgomery lived in South Carolina or across the Savannah River in Richmond County, Georgia. These included Zow (Tom Johnson), who lived in Aiken County; Manchuella (Katie Noble); Lucy Lanham and Cilucangy (Ward Lee), who lived in Edgefield; Mabiala (Uster Williams), who resided near Augusta; and Puka Geata (Tucker Henderson), who also lived in Richmond County. Two of them lived on land owned by Senator and former Governor Benjamin R. Tillman. One man, Cilucangy, was a noted basket weaver, and in 1904, he drafted a public appeal. He needed financial assistance, as he wanted to return to Africa. Sadly, his appeal was not successful, and Cilucangy never saw his homeland again.

Dark Days

Silence often veils slave life for South Carolina's "peculiar institution." Piecing together the dark picture of slavery on Edisto is complicated. Yet from personal recollections, oral interviews, newspaper accounts and public records, one catches glimpses of life behind the veil. A few of these glimpses hint at the pain slaves encountered in life.

For example, in 1865, the Freedmen's Bureau employed Mary Ann Ames and her friend Emily Bliss as teachers on Edisto Island. Ames interviewed her students about life before emancipation. One young man showed her "deep scars on his arms"—evidence of beatings. Apparently, at age eight, he rode one of the plantation horses to a distant location. Unfortunately for the young adventurer, a foal followed the horse and was lost. As a result, he was whipped.

Jessie Butler and Augustus Ladson interviewed Susie Hamilton (or Hamlin). Prior to emancipation, Hamilton and most of her family belonged to Edward Fuller. Fuller married Mary A. Mikell, an heiress from Edisto Island, and thereby acquired a large slave force, including Hamilton's family. Unfortunately, Hamilton's father was the property of another Edisto resident. From stories Hamilton heard, her father's master was "mean." In service, the father was a coachman. Apparently, one day, the father offended the master, who had him whipped. The following day, Hamilton's father drove his master about four miles from home, stopped and tied the man to a tree. The slave then in turn whipped his master, left him secured to the tree, untied the horse and ran to the boat landing. There, he jumped a coasting vessel and sailed

Freedmen's school, Edisto Island, Civil War era. New Englander Mary Ann Ames came to Edisto Island in order to educate the freedmen. *Samuel A. Cooley, photographer. Courtesy of Library of Congress, Prints & Photographs Division, LC-DIG-ppmsca-11194.*

to Charleston. In Charleston, the escaped slave successfully located a ship sailing to New York and signed on as crew. Despite other adventures, including being recognized by a friend of his owner's, the man apparently managed to live as a free man. Hamilton also remembered a laundress who was brutally whipped for attacking her mistress. According to Hamilton, when one slave was whipped, the other slaves were "made to watch."

DOMESTIC VIOLENCE

In November 1800, Dr. Samuel Fairchild petitioned the general assembly for payment. On June 21, 1800, a court of magistrates and freeholders convened on Edisto Island and tried Solomon, a slave belonging to Fairchild, for murder. Courts of magistrates and freeholders were ad hoc courts that tried cases involving slaves and free blacks. When a crime was reported, a magistrate would summon freeholders (landowners) from the area to hear the case. For Solomon's trial, John Hanahan and Richard Muncreef were

Aerial view of slave quarters, Seabrook plantation, Edisto Island, 1862. *Courtesy of Library of Congress, Prints & Photographs Division, LC-DIG-ppmsca-11378.*

the justices of the quorum, and the following Edisto residents were the freeholders: Benjamin Seabrook, William J. Mikell, William Edings, Daniel Townsend and Josiah Mikell.

After deliberation, the court found Solomon guilty of "wantonly and maliciously" killing Dorcas, his wife. That evening following the trial, Solomon was executed for the crime, and Fairfield petitioned for compensation. Under certain circumstances, the State of South Carolina compensated slave owners for slaves executed. The court had an appraisal made and directed the state treasurer in Charleston to pay Fairchild £65 sterling, the appraised value of Solomon. Yet months later, Fairchild still had not been paid. In addition to the overdue payment, Fairchild also wanted the legislature to consider compensating him for the loss of Dorcas. According to Fairchild, three "honest and worthy" residents of Edisto Island had valued her at £165. In 1800, Samuel Fairchild owned thirty-two slaves.

I. Jenkins Mikell's memoir also includes a domestic death. This murder occurred on the Mikell estate. A slave had hanged his wife from a rafter in their cabin. The murderer escaped to Charleston but was apprehended and returned. He was convicted and sentenced to execution. According to Mikell, the condemned man rode to the place of execution sitting on his coffin. As a witness, his paramour accompanied the condemned to his doom. After the execution, the murderer was buried on the plantation. According to Mikell, other slaves threatened to throw the mistress into the grave as well.

WHO KILLED BONAPARTE?

On May 27, 1816, Whitemarsh B. Seabrook summoned Dr. John King, a medical surgeon on Edisto Island, to attend an inquest. Seabrook, a justice of the peace on Edisto Island, convened a jury to investigate the death of Bonaparte, the property of William Hanahan. Before Bonaparte died, Samuel Hanahan had beaten the slave. King came as summoned, and with the jury as witnesses, he performed an "anatomical exposition of the Brain" of the deceased slave. The purpose of the inquest was to determine if Bonaparte had died from the blows struck by Samuel Hanahan. After observing the surgeon's exploration, the jury of inquest found that "the said negro man came to his death by some violent blows received on his head; and from the evidence before them, believe they were inflicted by Samuel Hanahan."

Although King testified before the grand jury in October, the grand jury did not return a true bill. Consequently, Samuel Hanahan was not prosecuted for the death of Bonaparte. According to the 1810 census, William Hanahan owned sixty-five slaves and Samuel Hanahan none. Dr. King, a native of England, immigrated to Charleston in 1803. In 1805, King married Mary Burden on Burden's Island, Colleton County. In 1816, Dr. King of Edisto Island performed a remarkable operation. He successfully removed an extra-uterine fetus and had the "rare good fortune" to save the lives of both mother and child.

CHICKENS COME HOME TO ROOST

In her *Tales of Edisto*, Nell S. Graydon recounted one story of slave abuse on Edisto. As the story goes, it was summer and the planters were at Edingsville. To punish a slave, the owner had him bound in a crouching position and displayed for all the other slaves to see. In Graydon's story, the owner paid for his crime in an unusual manner. In his old age, rheumatism afflicted the man so that he, too, was in a crouching position.

I. Jenkins Mikell in his memoir recounted the story of James, one of his personal minders. Although older than Mikell, the slave James was a young man. The slave's responsibility was to keep Mikell from overindulging on half-ripe plums, but he failed at this task. While Mikell was given an emetic, James was punished severely enough that he never allowed Mikell to "sin" again.

Corpus Delicti

The Edisto Militia had a role in one of the most controversial cases of antebellum Colleton District. On November 16, 1856, R.D.B. Walker petitioned the legislature for seventy-two dollars for services rendered Colonel H.W. Stewart of the Thirteenth Regiment. Governor John Lawrence Manning requested several militia companies to attend the executions of William Blackledge and Thomas Motley in Walterboro. Many feared an armed attack to rescue the accused. At their behest, in February 1854, Walker had served notice on the commanders of six companies of militia from Charleston, Colleton District and Edisto Island. Captain Murray commanded the Edisto Militia.

In 1853, Judge John Belton O'Neall presided over the court in Colleton District. Solicitor Milledge L. Bonham presented indictments against Thomas Motley, William Blackledge and Derril Rowell for the murder of a slave named Joe, "property of a person unknown." Due to time constraints, the court only heard the cases against Motley and Blackledge. The victim was an African American named Joe, either a slave or a free man but suspected by the defendants of being a runaway. In his defense, the man Joe always stated that his owner was a Manigault. In 1850, William Blackledge, a native of North Carolina, lived in Richland County with his twenty-two-year old wife and three small children. The thirty-five-year-old man listed no occupation. From testimony in the case, it appears that Blackledge and Motley were slave catchers—men who pursued runaways or captured suspected runaways. Owners, courts and even the state often offered compensation for the capture of such slaves. Motley's family also lived in Richland County.

As the testimony unfolded, on July 4, 1853, an individual named Grant apprehended Joe as a suspected runaway. That evening, Rowell and Blackledge called on Grant. At that time, Rowell took custody of Joe "until Grant could take him to jail" in Walterboro. On the following day, July 5, witnesses saw Joe in the custody of the three defendants, Rowell, Motley and Blackledge. The defendants also had several dogs with them. Onlookers heard the defendants call their prisoner "Joe." They also stated that they had whipped their prisoner because he did not name his owner but just repeated "that he belonged to Manigault." Witnesses testified that Motley and Blackledge treated Joe in a "cruel and barbarous" manner. In addition, two of the witnesses thought the treatment they observed was sufficient to kill the man. A physician concurred with that assessment.

According to testimony, Joe was "a black [man], hair very kinky, about five feet six inches high, and twenty-two years of age." The last time the witnesses saw Joe, he was alive and in the possession of the accused. Subsequently, circumstances suggested that Joe either escaped or was allowed to flee by the defendants. At that point, Rowell, Motley and Blackledge pursued—Motley on foot and Blackledge on horseback—the fugitive with their dogs and killed him.

In July, authorities arrested Motley and Blackledge. During questioning, Blackledge, with the expectation of immunity, confessed. Based on his confession, searchers found the "bones and hair of a Negro concealed behind a log in a swamp." After hearing the testimony, according to an unidentified source, a jury of slaveholders found both defendants guilty.

When he passed sentence, Judge O'Neall chided the defendants for the senseless, egregious cruelty they had shown "the poor begging unoffending slave." O'Neall refused to "repeat the disgusting details of the outrages" the men had inflicted on Joe. While the judge thought poverty would have motivated Blackledge, he found no excuse for Motley. According to O'Neall, Motley's father was a man of wealth, so there was no reasonable explanation for the young man being one hundred miles from home, "following a pack of dogs" and pursuing slaves through Lowcountry swamps. To the judge, Motley's conduct showed "either a love of cruelty, or of money." He sentenced the men to be hanged.

Attorneys for Motley and Blackledge appealed the convictions. Among other issues, they raised questions about the status of Joe, the possibility of manslaughter and Blackledge's confession. In January 1854, the court of appeals reviewed the case and considered the defense motions, but in the end, the justices dismissed Motley and Blackledge's motions for new trials.

The convictions of Motley and Blackledge stood. According to I. Jenkins Mikell, despite extensive "social and political pressure," the governor refused to commute the sentence.

After the court of appeals in Charleston dismissed their appeals and the governor refused to intervene, an armed guard accompanied Blackledge and Motley to Walterboro. Guards and the defendants returned aboard the *Colonel Myers*. Several detachments of militia joined a detachment of dragoons from Charleston to ensure that the execution was orderly. A little before noon on March 7, 1854, the prisoners were hanged in the yard of the Colleton District jail. According to witnesses, Blackledge and Motley were "humble and prepared for their fate." The Reverend Mr. Prentice, an Episcopal minister, accompanied the prisoners on their journey. Thomas Motley was the first prisoner executed, with his co-defender William Blackledge watching. Blackledge then asked for several modifications before he also faced the hangman. Blackledge left a wife and three children to mourn his fate. Although Motley was single, two of his brothers visited him in prison prior to the execution. Motley asked them to tell his parents that "he was comforted by the hope that he had made his peace with God." Both died without incident. Despite the governor's fears, there was no rescue attempt. According to Mikell, the militiamen encircled the scaffold and did not allow anyone near the execution. Some, he said, watched, but others looked away at the "gruesome spectacle." Once the sad affair ended, the various militia companies, including the men from Edisto, returned to their homes.

"Uncivil" Civil War

The Battle of Port Royal in November 1861 was a turning point for the Carolina Lowcountry. As a result of the successful amphibious assault, Union forces controlled Port Royal Harbor, the town of Beaufort, Hilton Head and many of the South Carolina Sea Islands. When they heard the news, most white planters fled their plantations. Some carried away

Steamboat Landing looking northward, July 2013. From Steamboat Creek, boats can easily use the North Edisto River to reach the Atlantic Ocean. Such access was a boon for smugglers. *Terry Helsley, photographer.*

personal property and attempted to relocate their slave property. Others fled in haste, abandoning their homes and slaves. Many also attempted to destroy their cotton crops. As part of this exodus, planters left Edisto Island. Consequently, the island was at times behind enemy lines and, more generally, a no-man's land. Union and Confederate foraging and scouting details occasionally clashed on the island. Gunboats patrolled the rivers, and the boom of ordnance at times disrupted the preternatural calm of the abandoned island.

EDISTO INSURRECTION

On January 20, 1862, according to General N.G. Evans, a group of blacks from Edisto Island attacked pickets near Watt's Cut. Evans asked Colonel P.F. Stevens to "capture the party and check the insurrection." He suspected Union troops had armed the attackers.

Consequently, on January 22, Colonel Stevens of the Holcombe Legion, CSA, led a detachment of 120 men across Dawhoo to Edisto Island. For this expedition, Reverend Baynard acted as Stevens's guide. The purpose of the expedition was to capture able-bodied slaves for work elsewhere; to locate and remove supplies, equipment and livestock; and to identify blacks who had attacked a Confederate picket. At William Whaley's plantation, the Confederates captured four slaves: Joe and his wife, an elderly couple left by Whaley; Bill, the property of W.G. Baynard, also "old and infirm"; and Peter, owned by Henry Seabrook and armed with a knife. Elsewhere on the island, Stevens's men seized ten other slaves. Near the Episcopal Church, the Confederates captured Paul (who belonged to the estate of James Clark) and his wife, Penny, and daughter Victoria, property of Henry Bailey. They took other slaves at Edward Whaley's plantation. But as the alarm had been given, some slaves escaped. Stevens and his forces moved across the island from plantation to plantation, rounding up the slaves living there. At the Legare and Seabrook plantations, four slaves were killed, drowned or wounded, including two women and a man who ran into the water and "were fired upon and disappeared beneath the water." A Union gunboat fired at the Confederates, and a party landed at Point of Pines. Stevens and his troops returned to Jehossee and later to the mainland. In addition to capturing about eighty men, women and children, Stevens "liberated" horses, mules, carts, wagons, corn and other provisions for Confederate service.

Freedmen, Hopkinson plantation, Edisto Island, 1862. *Courtesy of Library of Congress, Prints & Photographs Division, LC-DIG-ppmsca-11370.*

Headquarters of the First Massachusetts Cavalry, Edisto Island, 1862. *Henry P. Moore. Library of Congress, Prints & Photographs Division, LC-DIG-ppmsca-1134.*

Stevens suspected that the attackers were among the slaves captured. If the men were guilty, Stevens asked his commanding officer for permission to hang them. Stevens blamed the attack on Union activity in the area. Originally, Stevens planned to keep all the blacks in his custody and place the innocent in irons to build a causeway on James Island. Later, Stevens reported that he had sent the women and children to the workhouse in Charleston and that five of the men had confessed.

In March 1862, a Union soldier recounted entering the mouth of the North Edisto River past a "deserted rebel battery" near Botany Bay.

On April 5, 1862, Colonel Enoch Q. Fellows of the Third New Hampshire Volunteers reported that he and his troops had successfully occupied Edisto Island. After a reconnaissance of the island, Fellows and the Third Regiment settled on the island with two pieces of artillery. He expected the Forty-seventh New York Volunteers and the Fifty-fifth Pennsylvania Volunteers to reinforce his position. Union troops also shelled a suspected Confederate earthwork near Watt's Cut on Jehossee Island. With the arrival of Union forces, Confederate raids on Edisto temporarily ended.

HUTCHINSON AND BETRAYAL

For Edisto refugees, one of the most daunting events of the Civil War was the capture of a number of Edisto's young men, members of the famed "Rebel Troop." From Union sources, the story goes this way: on April 9, 1862, Acting Master J.C. Dutch of the U.S. bark *Kingfisher* reported that two contraband— James Hutchinson and William Bailey, former Edisto slaves—were on board under the master's protection. Hutchinson shared information with Dutch about Confederate pickets on Edisto Island. The pickets reported about the movements of Union gunboats and troops on the Edisto River and vicinity. Union troops then proceeded to Edisto and landed at Middleton's plantation. At the estate of Whaley (historian Charles Spencer identifies the site as Tom Seabrook's house), Dutch and his men captured nine Confederate cavalrymen and their arms. The Confederates captured were all Edisto men: Sergeant Townsend Mikell, Robert E. Seabrook, J.J. Wescoat, Alonzo Lee, Whitmarsh S. Murray, William B. Whaley, Frank Bailey, Joseph Edings and William G. Baynard. All the captives were privates with the Third South Carolina Regiment. Dutch sent the captives to Port Royal. One of the Confederates, Sydney Wescoat, escaped as he was stationed elsewhere. Union forces sent the captured Confederates north to Virginia. Shortly thereafter, they were exchanged and returned to South Carolina.

The diary of young Arthur Brailsford Wescoat shares the Confederate perspective. With the firing on Fort Sumter, Wescoat and his family left Edisto Island and sought refuge in Pinopolis. There, although too young to enlist, Wescoat accompanied his brother on exploratory expeditions. The brother was a corporal with the Rebel Troop. Later, young Wescoat joined the Stono Scouts. In January 1863, he accompanied Major John Jenkins to reconnoiter Edisto Island, where he ate oranges and commented on Union men buried before his church. The reconnaissance force camped at the home of T.P. Mikell on January 14. The Confederates sent parties not only to spy on the enemy but also to acquire livestock. Several entries in Wescoat's journal mention shooting cattle and trapping hogs. On April 13, Wescoat learned the identities of the men seized on Edisto: Townsend Mikell, Corporal Robert Seabrook, Whitmarsh Murray, Frank Bailey, Joseph Edings, William Baynard, Alonzo Lee, Joseph Wescoat and W. Whaley. Several of the men had their black servants with them. They were captured as well.

On April 15, 1862, Confederate cavalrymen hidden near Seabrook's plantation fired on an unarmed Union boat in the North Edisto River trying to salvage cotton from the brig *Empire*, which had run aground. As a result, Acting Master W.D. Urann of the U.S. gunboat *Crusader* was severely wounded in the right arm and left hand. A landing party of sixty men from the gunboat, including men from the Forty-seventh New York, Fifty-fifth Pennsylvania and Third New Hampshire, pursued the attackers. The two forces skirmished for twenty minutes or so at the Seabrook plantation. Eventually, howitzer fire dispersed the Confederate attackers, and the Union men returned to their ship.

In May 1862, a Union gunboat captured a Confederate battery at the juncture of the Dawhoo and Edisto Rivers. With the approach of the gunboat, battery defenders fled, abandoning their ordnance.

The Union troops left Edisto in the summer of 1862, so Confederates moved in to investigate the situation. Under orders from General Johnson Hagood, on August 18, Major John Jenkins with the Rebel Troop set out to reconnoiter Edisto Island. Jenkins left Adams Run and used flats to cross the Edisto River. Jenkins and his men landed on Jehossee Island and crossed the hastily rebuilt bridge over Watt's Cut. The men of the Rebel Troop visited plantations along their way as they headed toward the sea. Stopping at Seabrook's, from an upstairs window, Jenkins spotted ten men leaving a gunboat anchored off Point of Pines and coming ashore. Suspecting a foraging party, Jenkins and his men rushed to intercept. The Confederates fired on the men and captured

William Seabrook House (south elevation), Edisto Island. *C.O. Greene, photographer, September 1940. Courtesy of Library of Congress, Prints & Photographs Division, Historic American Buildings Survey, HABS SC,10-EDIL, 2-1.*

two Federal sailors: Carpenter, an engineer, and Hornsby, a captain's mate. The latter was severely wounded in his hand. Jenkins sent the prisoners inland. The rest of the party escaped. Jenkins and his force visited all the plantations on Edisto and toured the houses at Edingsville.

By 1865, the island was in Union hands. Yet as Mary Ann Ames, a northern teacher, noted in her diary, two companies of the Thirty-second Regulars, a black infantry regiment, were stationed on Edisto Island in 1865 to protect the area from guerrillas. She also reported that during her year on the island, authorities captured several marauders.

A CHRISTMAS TRAGEDY

Not all Civil War–related casualties on Edisto Island were military in nature. The Freedmen's Bureau and other organizations sent teachers and missionaries to the South Carolina Lowcountry to educate and minister to the freedmen. Among those serving on Edisto was James Pierpont Blake, superintendent of

Session house, Presbyterian Church on Edisto Island. *Courtesy of Library of Congress, Prints & Photographs Division, HABS SC,10-EDIL.*

freedmen's schools on the island and an attorney. Blake was the nephew of Eli Whitney, the inventor of the cotton gin, which played a major role in the expansion of short-staple cotton production across South Carolina and the Gulf states. Blake, a Yale College graduate, was crippled by polio.

On Christmas Day 1865, Blake and two female teachers, Ellen S. Kempton and Elmira B. Staton, crossed St. Pierre Creek to celebrate with friends. The New England Freedmen's Aid Society of Boston had sent Staton and Kempton to teach on Edisto Island. The twenty-five-year-old Kempton was a native of New Bedford, Massachusetts, and a teacher by occupation.

Sadly, on the return trip, within sight of the landing, the small boat capsized, and Blake and his companions died in St. Pierre Creek. Blake, due to his disability, was unable to swim, and the women did not know how. Despite a quick relief effort, as Mary Ames wrote, "only the hats and cloaks of the girls were found floating near the spot." In time, the bodies were recovered, and the three friends are buried in the churchyard of the Presbyterian Church on Edisto Island. The following marks their grave site:

> *In Memoriam*
> *"They were lovely and pleasant in their lives,*
> *And in death they were not divided."*

In another twist that Hollywood cannot rival, Daniel H. Chamberlain, a friend and Yale classmate of Blake, came to South Carolina to settle Blake's estate. Chamberlain later served as the best and last of the Reconstruction governors of South Carolina. In 1876, he lost a hotly contested controversial bid for reelection to former Confederate general Wade Hampton III. Hampton's victory signaled the end of Reconstruction in South Carolina.

In the March 1887 edition of *New Englander and Yale Review*, Chamberlain wrote of his friend: "There rest today beneath the moss-decked oaks of Edisto Island the remains of one young man, a brilliant child of New Haven and a class-mate of my own, whose life was lost—say rather, given—in the then 'forlorn hope' of negro education at the south."

Perils of Freedom

The Emancipation Proclamation and the end of the Civil War officially brought freedom to the formerly enslaved workers of Edisto Island and across the South. Many began to cultivate land near their homes. Unfortunately for the workers, their dream of independence and landownership was short-lived.

Hope and Betrayal

Under General William T. Sherman's January 1865 order, the freedmen on Edisto and elsewhere in the Lowcountry of South Carolina expected access to the plantations abandoned by their former owners. In addition, General O.O. Howard supported the freedmen's aspirations. So when President Andrew Johnson pardoned the former owners and ordered the land returned, Howard personally came to share the sad news with the workers on Edisto Island.

According to Mary Ames, twenty freedmen mounted on horses and mules formed two lines at the landing and saluted Howard and General Rufus Saxton as they walked through the formation. Such attentiveness and respect made Howard's job more difficult. The church was filled with black residents to hear Howard. The general explained that the president had pardoned the former owners and allowed them to reclaim their land. At first, as Ames

Dock, Seabrook plantation, 1862. Docks were lifelines for Edisto residents. *Courtesy of Library of Congress, Prints and Photographs Division, LC-DIG-ppmsca-11374.*

noted, the assembled group sat in stunned silence. Then, as the realization hit that they must "give up their little homes and gardens" and once more work for white men, there was "a general murmur of dissatisfaction." The men and women in attendance sang "Nobody Knows the Trouble I See" and "Wandering in the Wilderness of Sorrow and Gloom." The lyrics reflected their deep sense of loss and betrayal.

The devastated freedmen wrote letters of protest to Howard and President Johnson. Writing on behalf of "the people" in October 1865, a committee composed of Henry Bram, Ishmael Moultrie and Yates Sampson eloquently pleaded, "Will the good and just government take from us all this right and make us Subject to the will of those who have cheated and Oppressed us for many years." According to the committee, freedmen on Edisto Island had already taken up sixteen thousand acres and were ready to pay for the land. "This is our home," the men contended and asked for "a Homestead right here in the Heart of South Carolina." According to the 1870 census, Ishmael Moultrie was a twenty-nine-year-old clergyman living on Edisto Island.

Melton R. Linton, a member of the Thirty-fifth Regiment, shared his perspective in a letter dated "Edisto Island, March 26, 1866." Linton stated that he hoped "soon to be called a citizen of the U.S., and have the rights of a citizen." In December 1865, the secretary of state had declared that the Thirteenth Amendment to the United States Constitution had been ratified. The Thirteenth Amendment abolished slavery in the United States. As a future citizen, Linton was "opposed…to working under a contract." From Linton's point of view, he had as much right to hire a white man as a white man had to hire him. Linton planned to remain in South Carolina a year after his enlistment ended. He did not want to "hire" himself out to a planter, as he had "seen some men hired who were turned off without being paid." Linton continued, "They [white residents] try to pull us down faster than we can climb up. They have no reason to say that we will not work, for we raised them, and sent them to school." From his vantage point, Linton thought that "it is as little as they can do to give us some of their land." Linton's opinion appeared in the *South Carolina Leader*, an African American newspaper.

RIOT

As a result of these land issues, conflicts and communication issues arose between the landowners and the newly freed workforce. For example, on the Fourth of July 1869, black residents of Edisto Island protested the conditions of their work contracts. According to published reports, planters had offered the workers approximately five acres of land to cultivate personally in exchange for two days' work (Monday and Tuesday) each week. The workers accepted the terms and worked without incident until Independence Day. In 1868, the Fourth of July fell on a Sunday. Consequently, as Sunday was the day of worship, the workers expected to celebrate the holiday on Monday. The landowners objected and demanded that the workers compensate them by laboring another day during the week. Many workers refused, so the owners obtained writs of ejectment against the workers. As a result, legal authorities ejected several of the workers from their land. Among them was Cyrus Haywood. Haywood, like the others, had devoted "much time" to cultivating and improving his plot, so he found the ejectment "unreasonable" and returned to his allotment.

In turn, the planters requested and acquired another writ. When Constable Marstella appeared to once again evict Haywood, Haywood refused to leave. The constable then threatened to forcibly remove him. Haywood objected to the constable's methods. While Haywood was willing to leave, he did not want to be tied up "like a calf," bound hand and foot and tossed into a cart. Yet the constable and his assistants persisted, and Haywood resisted. In the fray, someone shot Haywood through the hand. Afterward, the constable and his men trussed up Haywood, threw the wounded man into a cart and

Bean pickers, Edisto Island. *Photograph WPA–AB-4. Courtesy of the South Caroliniana Library, University of South Carolina, Columbia.*

then carried him to the magistrate's. The magistrate, in turn, imprisoned Haywood, refused to dress his wound and left him in solitary confinement for three days. After three days, with the help of friends, Haywood escaped.

The news of Haywood's arrest spread quickly. Friends and associates on the island gathered to support Haywood and protest his arrest. Approximately 150 persons, some armed, converged on the homes of the magistrate and constable and demanded Haywood's release. A few even threatened to harm the officers if their demands were not met. Eventually, the crowd, convinced that Haywood was gone, dispersed.

The next week, Sheriff E.W. Mackey and two detectives arrived on Edisto to arrest five men who had allegedly abetted Haywood's escape and spearheaded the protest movement. However, the men—Peter P. Hedges, Alfred Smith, Moses Brown, Boston Jenkins and Moses Gadsden— surrendered without incident. Mackey and his men conveyed them to Charleston, where they were arraigned. According to the 1870 census,

Gadsden (age forty-eight), Jenkins (age fifty) and Brown (age twenty-six) were field laborers on Edisto Island. In 1868, Haywood, Hedges and Brown were also registered voters.

The incident ended peacefully. Thanks to the efforts of the sheriff, both sides compromised. On one side, the Edisto workers returned to their homes and made up the missed day of work. And on the other side, the planters withdrew their legal action to eject the workers. Reflecting a typical South Carolina perspective—particularly of the time—the news account clearly blamed the intransigence of northern landowners for the dispute, contending that island blacks preferred to work for southern planters.

THE PRICE OF A LIFE

James Geraty (b. 1842) was the son of Christopher (1815–1892) and Ann Geraty (1819–1867). Both of his parents were natives of Ireland. In 1843, Christopher Geraty filed notice of his intention to become a citizen. He was by trade a grocer. During the Civil War, he left Charleston (possibly during the bombardment) and, with his family, lived in Barnwell County. There, in January and February 1865, he encountered Union troops of the Seventeenth Army Corps under the overall command of General William T. Sherman. In 1871, Christopher Geraty applied to the Southern Claims Commission for compensation for property taken for use of the army. In his original claim, Geraty listed horses, mules, carts, a wagon, a harness, blankets, bedding, clothing, cattle, poultry, an English saddle and thousands of pounds of bacon and flour for a total value of $6,860. Geraty's list suggests that he operated a store in Barnwell at the time. Geraty revised his claim and reapplied in 1878. In order to receive compensation, the claimant had to affirm his loyalty to the Union. While Geraty listed several witnesses in Charleston and Barnwell to testify to his loyalty to the Union, the commission disallowed Geraty's claims. According to Geraty's file, his name appeared on the rolls of Captain J.F. O'Neill's Company A, First Regiment, South Carolina Reserves, with the rank of fourth sergeant. As a Confederate soldier, Geraty was not eligible for compensation.

James Geraty and his brother William Christopher Geraty also worked as grocers. According to a newspaper account, at one point, James Geraty had studied for the priesthood. But ill health ended that pursuit, and Geraty returned to Charleston and the family business. According to the *Charleston City Directory* of 1869–70, James Geraty operated a grocery at 22 South Bay Street in Charleston. When his mother died in 1867, her address was 25 South Bay Street. At some point after the death of Ann Geraty, the family relocated, and in 1870, James and his family lived with his father, Christopher Geraty, on Wadmalaw Island. According to the census, Christopher, James and W.C. Geraty—the three adult male members of the household—were all grocers. The census entry suggests that the Geraty family had either relocated their grocery or expanded their operations. By 1875, James Geraty operated a grocery store on Edisto Island at Townsend Mikell's plantation. At the time of his death, James and his wife, Mary (1841–1897), were the parents of three children: George P., James W. and Agnes Alma.

On February 24, 1875, around 8:00 p.m., a group of boatmen entered Geraty's store. The men selected merchandise worth about four dollars but then asked for credit. When Geraty refused their request for credit, the men attempted to remove the goods by force. Geraty resisted, and one of the men struck him on the head with a club that had an iron spike imbedded in it. Geraty died instantly. Like Gilling, another man's dream of commercial success on Edisto ended in tragedy.

Dr. Daniel T. Pope and John King, trial justice "acting as coroner" on Edisto Island, filed Geraty's death certificate. Authorities transported Geraty's body to Charleston. Geraty is buried with his parents and other family members in St. Lawrence Cemetery, Charleston.

After investigation, authorities promptly arrested John Smith and charged him with the murder of Geraty. Smith confessed his guilt and was tried, convicted and sentenced to death. Consequently, authorities hanged the twenty-four-year-old Smith in the yard of the county jail in Charleston. On July 30, 1875, Aaron Logan, Charleston County coroner, certified the death of John Smith. According to the *New York Tribune*, "several thousand persons" witnessed the execution. Smith's accomplice, Joe Gibbs, was more fortunate. Although sentenced to execution, Gibbs received a last-minute reprieve. Lieutenant Governor Richard Howell Gleaves—acting for South Carolina governor Daniel H. Chamberlain, who was out of state at the time—commuted Gibbs's sentence from death to twenty years in prison. Gleaves, a native of Philadelphia, was a business partner of Robert Smalls in Beaufort. As South Carolina's only black lieutenant governor, Gleaves served from December 7, 1872, to December 14, 1876.

STATUS QUO ANTEBELLUM

According to *Harper's Weekly*, in the fall of 1878, the Democratic commissioners on Edisto Island refused to open the polls. As a result, residents could not vote. In a few Lowcountry counties with large black majorities, black candidates still enjoyed limited success at the polls, but the tide had turned. During the Reconstruction years (roughly 1868 to 1876), black South Carolinians voted and held political office. This great opportunity for black representation and education ended in 1876. That year, white South Carolinians seized control of the state government and elected former Confederate general Wade Hampton governor. Hampton's election "redeemed" the state and reestablished white control. This action in 1878 suggests that Edisto Island was the scene of uncertainty and agitation. Not all former black voters quietly accepted efforts to limit their voting opportunities and restrict their civil rights.

Death and Mystery

The post-Reconstruction years were difficult for South Carolina's black residents. From 1876 to 1900, Jim Crow legislation spread legal segregation across the state. This effort culminated in 1895 with a new state constitution that severely limited black voting rights and virtually eliminated black political participation.

JAMES HUTCHINSON

According to Sam Gadsden, at one time, Edisto had two "black kings": James "Jim" Hutchinson and John Thorne. Thorne was a successful businessman. He owned over three hundred acres of land, had a commodious dwelling, ran a store and operated a commercial cotton gin. In addition, Thorne shared his success and supplied capital to other black farmers.

While Thorne was a businessman, Hutchinson was a political activist. Jim Hutchinson was precinct chair of the Republican Party on Edisto Island, and during Reconstruction, he organized black voters. Hutchinson also understood the value of self-sufficiency and promoted black ownership of land. In 1870, he wrote Governor Robert Scott asking the governor's assistance in acquiring land on Edisto Island. According to Hutchinson's petition, at a mass meeting, island blacks had requested his help in acquiring a nine-hundred-acre plantation on Edisto Island. As Hutchinson noted, "We need this land."

Agricultural workers planting Irish potatoes, Edisto Island, circa 1939. *Carl T. Julien, photographer. Photograph WPA-T-AB5. Courtesy of the South Caroliniana Library, University of South Carolina, Columbia.*

The Edisto residents wanted the governor or his agent to purchase the land and then allow them to repay the purchase price. In closing, Hutchinson reminded the governor of their support: "We have stood by and supported you throughout this last campaign almost to a man…We would not have done so had we not believed you were a gentleman of principle having the good of the poorer classes in view as well as that of the rich." Although Scott's response is not known, Hutchinson remained a Republican.

In 1872, Hutchinson and other Edisto residents pooled their resources and formed an association. The participants then executed an agreement to acquire land on the island and divide it into nineteen shares. Certain Edisto residents—Joseph Whaley, Caesar Graham, Sandy Simmons, Mathew Johnson, Primus Green, Titus Finley, Brister Brown, August Deas, William Fickling, Edward Galloway and Frank Watson—purchased one to two shares and appointed James Hutchinson their agent. Per the agreement, Hutchinson reserved three shares for himself and his heirs. Hutchinson then purchased the 234-acre plantation known as Seaside for $2,000 from Augustine T. Smythe. As referee of the court of common pleas, Smythe sold the property as the result of a suit in equity brought by *Joseph S. Legare v. Francis Legare.*

As Gadsden notes, Hutchinson "got land for poor people." According to deeds filed in Charleston, he purchased land on Edisto, subdivided the tracts and resold the land in smaller parcels. Hutchinson, like Thorne, was a leader of black island residents and an advocate for black rights. Hutchinson and Thorne cooperated to secure land and opportunities for black residents.

Hutchinson was a Civil War veteran who served in the United States navy from 1863 to 1865. In 1866, an agent of the Bureau of Refugees, Freedmen and Abandoned Lands issued a land certificate to James Hutchinson under owner William Edings at Seaside. Born circa 1834, in 1880, Hutchinson was a forty-nine-year-old farmer at the time. His household included Rachel, his wife; and his seventy-year-old mother, Maria. According to Charles Spencer, Hutchinson may have been the son of Isaac Jenkins Mikell. According to the 1880 agricultural census, Hutchinson owned fifty improved acres and seventy unimproved. On February 3, 1875, C.C. Bowen, sheriff of Charleston County, wrote Governor Daniel H. Chamberlain recommending worthy candidates to be appointed trial justice. Among others, Bowen recommended Hutchinson (already known to the governor) because "gratitude prompts his recommendation and demands his appointment."

Then, one fateful day, according to Sam Gadsden, a white man from Wadmalaw "whose brother used to run the store by where the Post Office is now" on Store Creek killed Hutchinson. At the time, there was a meeting (possibly political) at the Hutchinson house. Apparently, the presence of the assailant was neither expected nor wanted. The unidentified man approached the house and engaged Hutchinson in conversation. At that point, Hutchinson vehemently ordered the interloper off his land. Before running away, the man shot and killed Hutchinson.

Hutchinson died in August 1882, the month and year of Sam Gadsden's birth. So Gadsden's account is not firsthand information but instead reflects preserved memories handed down from generation to generation. His memories support the assumption that Hutchinson's political prominence and history of activism were factors in his murder—a viable possibility. By the 1880s, the high tide of black political power had ebbed, and white leaders wanted to limit black political power, eliminate civil rights and restore social and political relations to pre–Civil War days. In such a context, Hutchinson was a dangerous man—a leader who commanded respect. He was a man with

Hutchinson House, July 2013. Henry Hutchinson, son of Jim Hutchinson, one of Edisto's "Black Kings," built this house for his bride, Rosa Swinton. *Jacob Helsley, photographer.*

a different worldview and a history of activism for the black inhabitants of the island. Gadsden's enigmatic statement, "The same politics that made Jim into a big man...was the thing that protected the killer," suggests a political power struggle. Hutchinson's advocacy for black civil and land rights made him a marked man. The 1880s were violent years in South Carolina. For example, in 1882, whites lynched six black men. By 1890, South Carolina reported three times the number of murders as all the New England states combined—even though their population outnumbered South Carolina's four to one. On Edisto, authorities never solved the Hutchinson murder, but as Gadsden noted, the black owners kept their land.

Henry Hutchinson, the reputed son of Jim Hutchinson, married Rosa Swinton in 1885. For his new bride, Hutchinson built a home on Point of Pines Road. In 1987, the house was listed on the National Register of Historic Places.

OTHER DEATHS

On July 4, 1915, James Brown of Edisto Island died from a "gunshot wound in the abdomen." Brown was twenty-two years old and was buried on the island.

In May 1924, a fight between two young men on Edisto Island ended badly. One fatally stabbed the other and was found guilty of manslaughter.

Afterward, the young man was sentenced to five years in the state reformatory. Also in 1924, Cyrus Gadsden was "found dead by the side of the Public Road" on Edisto Island. Dr. Jenkins W. Pope conducted an autopsy. On Christmas Eve 1925, Magistrate W.W. Anderson, as acting coroner, convened a jury to investigate Gadsden's death. The members of the jury were Arthur W. Bailey, James W. Kuger, James S. Clark, Fred Jenkins, Edward Simmons and Manny Campbell. After deliberation, the jury ruled that Gadsden died from "a Gun shot wound by Hand unknown to us, Supposed to be a Pistol or Rifle Ball, this Dec. 24th AD 1925."

Jinxed

One unexplained death in a family is a tragedy. Two such deaths are a catastrophe. Three would suggest the need for an exorcism. The McConkey family of Edisto Island faced more than their fair share of disasters. McConkeys were in Charleston in the late antebellum period, and family connections moved to Edisto after the Civil War.

Early McConkeys in Charleston

On March 5, 1849, the *Charleston Courier* carried an advertisement for Corner & McConkey, House & Sign Painters. The partners announced that they were relocating their business from 68 Church Street to 56 Meeting Street, "nearly opposite the Hibernian Hall." Corner and McConkey guaranteed to handle all orders promptly. Among their offerings were graining and special effects in kalsomine (whitewash) for ceilings and walls "warranted not to rub off."

In the 1850s, McConkey advertised several times for a "house painter." Either business was good or McConkey had difficulty keeping employees. On June 28, 1851, James and Alexander McConkey announced their co-partnership in the house painting business as J&A McConkey. Their business address was 56 Broad Street. James acquired several major painting contracts, including a "splendid edifice" that opened in 1852 on the corner of King and Market Streets and the Charleston theater.

James McConkey's life changed in 1860. On June 13, the *Charleston Mercury* carried a special notice. Edward Templeton and Thomas Necklin of 48 Broad Street announced their purchase of James McConkey's stock in trade, including "paints, French zinc and paper hangings." A few days later, McConkey ran an ad encouraging his friends and former customers to patronize the new partners. On June 20, James McConkey applied for a passport, perhaps to visit family abroad or for a business trip. By this time, he was already a naturalized citizen.

The great Charleston fire of 1861 damaged 68 Meeting Street, a property owned but not occupied by McConkey.

In addition to his business, James McConkey was involved in local politics. James and Alexander McConkey were brothers as well as business associates. In 1870, James McConkey is enumerated with two other painters—Tom Hicklin and Ed McDonald—suggesting a business relationship. In 1871, James's business address was 48 Broad Street.

On November 19, 1879, Alexander's wife, Annie, died of apoplexy on Edisto Island. Alexander predeceased her on June 17, 1872. His death certificate listed his occupation as "painter" and his address as 102 Broad Street, Charleston. The funeral notice invited friends of Mr. and Mrs. Alexander McConkey and his brother James to attend Alexander's service at the First Presbyterian Church. The deceased was a member of Burns Charitable Association.

The precise connection between the Charleston and Edisto McConkeys is unknown. According to the census, Alexander and Ann McConkey were born in Ireland, and from the death notice, Alexander and James were brothers. Nevertheless, the evidence suggests that they were related to the Canadian branch of the family.

THE McCONKEYS OF EDISTO ISLAND

The first McConkey landowner on Edisto Island was James McConkey, a Canadian. Pursuant to a court order to satisfy a debt, on March 23, 1874, C.C. Bowen, sheriff of Charleston County, conveyed Seaside to Thomas McConkey at a cost of $10,000. Subsequently, on April 7, 1874, Thomas McConkey executed a power of attorney in favor of James McConkey. By this document, Thomas McConkey of New York empowered James McConkey—who was, according to some sources, his nephew—to handle all matters concerning Thomas's purchase of "Sea Side," a plantation of 1,200 acres plus or minus on Edisto Island, including executing bonds and mortgages. In 1870, the census lists one Thomas McConkey, a thirty-eight-year-old inspector who lived in lodgings on West Thirty-sixth Street, New York City. But this Thomas may not be the one who purchased Seaside. By a deed of gift, in 1875, Thomas McConkey transferred title to Seaside to James McConkey. In 1892, James McConkey died on Edisto Island.

SEASIDE

Seaside was a plantation with a dark past. Originally known as Locksley Hall, according to Nell Graydon, even before the ill-fated McConkeys arrived, it was a "house of tragedy." According to family stories, several young children died of diphtheria, one owner committed suicide in an especially bloody manner and there were other deaths as well.

In 1880, the younger James McConkey owned the plantation on Edisto Island. In 1900, Janie McConkey (born in May 1856) was the head of the McConkey household on Edisto. Other household members included Rena (Erina) McConkey (born in August 1854), her sister, and the Seabrook family: George W. (born in January 1867), Minnie B. (born in October 1869), Alonzo

B. (born in March 1890) and George W. (born in June 1892). In a bizarre twist, Janie McConkey died of burns. According to Sam Gadsden, she "burnt up right in the yard." Janie McConkey was cooking on a stove in an outbuilding. Suddenly,

Seaside House (front view), vicinity of South Carolina Highway 174. McConkey's landholdings included Seaside and Edisto Beach. *Courtesy of the Library of Congress, Prints & Photographs Division, HABS SC, 10-EDIB.V, 1-2.*

engulfed in flames, she ran from the building. Onlookers tried to extinguish the flames, but she died a horrific death. Her will mentioned her uncle James; brothers John (in Cobb County, Georgia) and Robert (and his son James); and sisters Charlotte and Erina, although Erina had predeceased her, dying in 1904. The McConkeys, apparently, were a large clan.

According to the 1910 census, James McConkey (age forty-five) and his brother John (age thirty-eight) lived together on Edisto Island. Both were natives of Oxford, Ontario, Canada. Their father, Thomas, had emigrated from Ireland to Canada. George Washington "Washie" Seabrook managed Seaside plantation for the McConkeys.

Trinity Episcopal Church, Edisto Island, July 2013. Four McConkey siblings are buried in the Trinity churchyard. *Terry Helsley, photographer.*

Perhaps in an effort to diversify his investment, on April 19, 1914, James McConkey advertised in the *State* for a "tenant with capital for a store" on Edisto Island. McConkey guaranteed "good cash trade."

On November 22, 1915, John McConkey, age sixty-five, was murdered and robbed. According to his death certificate, his attacker(s) fractured his skull and cut his throat. Early newspaper accounts reported that McConkey was a "prominent farmer." On November 23, a servant found McConkey's body at the stables. Despite efforts of law enforcement officers, they found no trace of the culprit. Initially, officials considered robbery the motive and thought McConkey had died around 11:00 p.m. Monday night. Apparently, McConkey had planned to travel to Charleston but arrived at the landing too late to catch the steamer. He talked a while with Dr. J.O. Lea, and then around 9:00 p.m., he left for home. There, party or parties unknown ambushed and killed McConkey while he was stabling his mule. The drive from the landing to Seaside normally took two hours.

Above, left: Tombstone of John McConkey: "Erected to the memory of John McConkey who was so cruelly murdered November 23, 1915 aged 60 years." Trinity Episcopal Church, Edisto Island, January 2014. *Terry Helsley, photographer.*

Above, right: Tombstone of Jane, or Janie, McConkey (May 1856–January 6, 1912), who tragically burned to death. Trinity Episcopal Church, Edisto Island, January 2014. *Terry Helsley, photographer.*

The news account also noted that, in addition to the other injuries, the attacker(s) broke McConkey's jawbone. The extent and nature of the wounds suggested a violent, angry attack. Although his pockets were rifled through, his watch was untouched. Despite this fact, law enforcement continued to consider McConkey's death a robbery gone wrong.

Sheriff J. Elmore Martin and Rural Policemen Beckett and Henderson traveled from Charleston to Edisto in an effort to apprehend the murderer of John McConkey. On November 27, Sheriff Martin and Coroner John G. Mansfield arrested six black residents on Edisto Island and jailed them in Charleston. According to the *State*, the sheriff identified Jonah (his name also appears as James) Gadsden Jr. and April Bailey as probable culprits. He also jailed Billy and Johnny Williams, Robert Lawrence and

Elijah Simmons as witnesses. The accused men had formerly worked for McConkey. In addition to the accused, the officials "brought an axe, sticks of heavy wood and a lantern covered with blood." In February 1916, the Charleston County Court of General Sessions considered the indictment of James Gadsden and April Bailey, charged with the murder of John McConkey.

John McConkey's funeral was on November 24, and afterward, he was buried in Trinity Episcopal churchyard on Edisto Island. Survivors included brothers and a sister in Ontario. John McConkey died intestate. Apparently, his brother Thomas of Lakeside, Ontario, represented the family. The court appointed J.O. Lea and George Washington Seabrook to administer the estate.

The death of John McConkey continues to be a matter of interest. Several published accounts share residents' memories and oral traditions. Sam Gadsden, for example, paints a picture of a doomed family—James dying, Erina dying, Janie burning to death and John being murdered. According to Gadsden, the McConkeys were not good farmers, and at the time John McConkey died, Mitchell Seabrook and Wash Seabrook managed the farm. According to Gadsden, the workers at Seaside "had the idea" that the Seabrooks were involved in McConkey's death. After the death of McConkey, the Seabrooks eventually acquired Seaside, and according to Clara Puckette, in the 1920s, Mitchie Seabrook and G. Washington Seabrook began to develop Edisto Beach.

John G. Murray had another perspective. Exonerating the Seabrooks, he enigmatically stated that "another white man" killed McConkey. Nevertheless, as the man was never charged and the case against him was never proven, Murray saw no reason to share the name. Murray's statements suggest that some Edisto residents knew more about McConkey's death than was ever officially acknowledged.

Opposite, top: Tombstone of James McConkey (October 24, 1823–July 14, 1892), brother of John McConkey, and their sister Erina McConkey (August 16, 1844–March 5, 1904), Trinity Episcopal Church, Edisto Island, January 2014. Although they died at different times, this stone has inscriptions for both siblings. *Terry Helsley, photographer.*

Opposite, bottom: Seaside House, Edisto Island. John McConkey and his siblings owned Seaside plantation. *Courtesy of Library of Congress, Prints & Photographs Division, HABS SC, 10-EDIB.V,1-1.*

McConkey's Jungle Shack, Jungle Road, Edisto Beach, December 2013. The name of the popular eatery honors the area's history. Edisto Beach was once known as McConkey Beach. *Terry Helsley, photographer.*

McConkey's Seaside included the Edisto Beach State Park as well as Seaside plantation. Edisto Beach was named in honor of McConkey until 1970. In 2007, McConkey's Jungle Shack opened on Jungle Road. The restaurant's name commemorates an earlier tragic chapter in the island's history.

Price of Petulance

Crime, scandal and death darkened Edisto's history. But not all dark days reflected the sordid vicissitudes of human frailties. In the 1950s, Edisto was the stage for a different drama when tradition clashed with law. The 1950s were turbulent years in American history as African Americans marched, protested and sued for civil rights and equal opportunities. South Carolinians from Clarendon County were plaintiffs (*Briggs v. Elliott*) in the historic *Brown v. Board of Education* case decided by the United States Supreme Court on May 17, 1954. This landmark decision declared that the doctrine of "separate but equal" as applied to public education was inherently unequal. With this decision, residents of the United States turned from segregation to integration. Subsequent cases addressed other public facilities.

In South Carolina, one of the public facilities that came under scrutiny was Edisto Beach State Park. South Carolina's state park system was a product of the 1930s. With the country's economy in ruins, President Franklin D. Roosevelt promoted a number of New Deal programs. The Civilian Conservation Corps (CCC), one of these New Deal programs, offered employment opportunities for young men. Under the aegis of the CCC, workmen established camps and developed parks, such as Poinsett State Park and Hunting Island State Park, across the state. In April 1935, the *State* reported that a CCC camp and state park on Edisto Beach were "an assured fact." Development began in the summer of 1935. The camp occupied two sites: one on the beach and the other on higher ground behind the shore.

Vacation cabin, Edisto State Park. Edisto Beach State Park is one the most visited South Carolina parks. *South Carolina Commission of Forestry, Photograph WPA-PL-CH-EI-11. Courtesy of the South Caroliniana Library, University of South Carolina, Columbia.*

CCC workmen erected no-frills cabins with minimum amenities that were rented to tourists. They also cleared underbrush, built roads and walking paths and addressed insect control. In addition, CCC employees developed and implemented soil and forest conservation programs. As the newspaper reported, the site was a "barrier island, once known as McConkey's or Big Bay." Edisto Beach was chosen as a park site because of its elevation, location and perceived insulation from hurricane damage.

Such a delightful spot naturally attracted attention from residents on the island and throughout the state. Although several South Carolina state parks—for example, Hunting Island—had separate facilities for black and white visitors, Edisto, despite the island's large black population, did not. Consequently, in 1961, some Carolinians filed a class-action suit in the United States District Court in Charleston. The suit sought to integrate South Carolina's twenty-three state parks and open such public amenities to all Carolinians. At the time of the suit, five of the twenty-three parks were designated for black residents and eighteen for white. The South Carolina State Commission of Forestry administered South Carolina's parks. Plaintiffs sought to desegregate the parks, contending "that a South Carolina law requiring segregation in state parks is unconstitutional," as it "denies the equal protection and due process guaranteed by the Fourteenth Amendment."

Palmettos and boat on beach, Edisto Island. *Carl T. Julien, photographer. Photograph WPA-PL-CO-8. Courtesy of the South Caroliniana Library, University of South Carolina, Columbia.*

The 1961 federal suit followed earlier efforts to integrate Edisto Beach State Park. J. Arthur Brown, a Charleston resident and in 1961 president of the South Carolina chapter of the National Association for the Advancement of Colored People (NAACP), spearheaded the effort. In 1953, Arthur J. Clement Jr. issued the opening volley in the struggle. Clement wrote the

Sand and surf, Edisto Beach State Park, January 2014. *Terry Helsley, photographer.*

Charleston legislative delegation asking for its assistance in allowing blacks to use the Edisto park. Two years later, on May 12, 1955, Brown wrote Donald B. Cooler, superintendent of Edisto Beach State Park, requesting permission to visit the park. Cooler's reply, dated May 21, 1955, stated that the "park was established in 1935 for the exclusive use of white persons, and based on custom and precedents we will have to deny your request." As a result, in 1956, with the support of the Charleston NAACP, Etta Clark, whose child attended Avery Institute, and others filed suit to desegregate Edisto Beach State Park. That case, *Etta Clark, et al v. C.H. Flory, State Forester, et al*, was filed in United States District Court in Charleston. According to Edmund Drago, the case progressed through the courts, but the "issue became moot because the South Carolina Commission of Forestry closed the beach entirely."

On February 10, 1956, the South Carolina State Commission of Forestry, rather than consider integration, closed Edisto Beach State Park. Edisto Beach State Park, according to the *New York Times*, was the "first public facility ordered closed in the state as a result of the segregation crisis." In other instances, the state chose other avenues of resistance. For example, in order to avoid integration, officials leased golf and other public park amenities to private groups.

The district court dismissed the 1956 suit, but as historian Stephen Lewis Cox noted, the Edisto park case was important because of "the strategies and lessons learned by both sides." These strategies and lessons eventually produced later victories. Nevertheless, the park was still closed at the time of the 1961 suit. In July 1961, the federal district court ordered South Carolina to open state parks. Yet the matter continued until U.S. judge J. Robert Martin ruled positively in a 1963 discrimination suit and gave the Forestry

Bateaux at the dock, Edisto Beach State Park, 1951. *Beulah Glover, photographer. Photograph 12239.31. Courtesy of the South Caroliniana Library, University of South Carolina, Columbia.*

Edisto Beach State Park, January 2014. Efforts to desegregate Edisto Beach State Park eventually opened South Carolina's parks to all residents. *Terry Helsley, photographer.*

Commission until September 8, 1963, to integrate. Instead, the Forestry Commission closed all South Carolina state parks. Although the parks reopened the following year with limited access, the issue continued to fester.

Matters came to a head on the anniversary of American independence. On July 4, 1965, an integrated group of thirteen college and high school students arrived at Edisto Beach State Park to picnic and swim. Shortly after the "Edisto 13" unpacked, authorities arrested them for "trespassing on public property" and "disturbing the peace." Magistrate W.E. Seabrook sentenced each to pay a fine of fifty dollars or serve thirty days in jail. The defendants appealed and posted bond pending trial in Charleston. Among the protestors arrested were Dennis Barrett and David Lawlor, law interns for the NAACP in Charleston, and Marian Bennett, a teacher in a Charleston Head Start program. Bennett was the daughter of L. Howard Bennett, assistant to the deputy assistant secretary of defense for civilian personnel, industrial relations and civil rights. L. Howard Bennett, a native of South Carolina, was the first African American judge in Minnesota. A lawyer and civil rights activist, Bennett served in the United States Defense Department under President John F. Kennedy. Defending the students were attorneys Matthew Perry, Bernard Fielding and Russell Brown. Perry was later appointed South Carolina's first black federal judge.

Finally, on June 20, 1966, South Carolina shifted gears and completely integrated the parks and all park facilities. The long battle for equal access to state park facilities that began on Edisto ended in victory for all South Carolinians.

Unusual and Unexplained Deaths

Fred Robinson's Death

In 1989, the Southern Poverty Law Center dedicated the Civil Rights Memorial in Montgomery, Alabama, which listed the names of forty "civil rights martyrs." As part of the center's research, employees compiled information concerning seventy-four possibly racially motivated deaths between 1952 and 1968. The memorial does not list all the names, as adequate information about the circumstances of their deaths was not available. Nevertheless, the center identified these individuals at the Civil Rights Center as "The Forgotten." One of those forgotten individuals is Fred Robinson. According to the center, Fred Robinson died on Edisto Island in 1960, and the condition of Robinson's body suggested foul play. According to the center, when Robinson's body washed ashore on August 5, "his eyes were reportedly gouged out and his skull crushed."

In March 2007, the FBI and United States Department of Justice announced that they were reexamining three civil rights–era cases in South Carolina. The three cases were the Orangeburg Massacre in 1968, the death of James Waymers in Allendale County in 1965 and the death of Fred Robinson of Edisto Island in 1960. Investigators explored the cases to see if the evidence warranted reopening the cases. Later, in November 2011, the Federal Bureau of Investigation announced that "Civil Rights era prosecutions are nearly over."

As there is no statute of limitation on murder, the Department of Justice, under its "Cold Case Initiative" and the Emmett Till Unsolved Civil Rights Crime Act of 2007, studied 111 incidents involving 124 deaths. In two-thirds of the cases, the department notified the victims' families that the government had pursued their cases as far as possible. In rare instances, there were prosecutions. The Justice Department and FBI faced challenges trying to ascertain if the crimes were "racially motivated" and, if so, "whether there was anyone alive to prosecute." Nevertheless, at that time, there were still 39 "officially open" cases. One of these was the death of Fred Robinson.

Robinson's Death Certificate

Yet Robinson's death certificate filed with the South Carolina Department of Health and Environmental Control tells a different story. According to his death certificate, Fred, or Freddie, Robinson was born on January 15, 1948, and died at 3:30 p.m. on August 3, 1960. His mother, Lavenia Robinson, listed his occupation as "student." The Robinsons lived on Edisto Island. At the time of his death, Fred Robinson was only twelve years old. Exactly what happened that day is unclear. Yet on August 9, the coroner signed a death certificate ruling Robinson's death accidental. According to the coroner, Robinson drowned after he "fell overboard while playing on Lybrand's dock, located on Big Bay creek, Edisto Island." Fielding Funeral

Big Bay Creek, January 2014. Young Fred Robinson died in an accident at Lybrand's dock on Big Bay Creek. *Terry Helsley, photographer.*

Home handled the funeral arrangements for the family, and on August 7, Robinson was buried in the cemetery of First Baptist Church, Edisto Island.

ICARUS

On March 2, 1933, Merrell B. King fell from the sky. He plummeted eight hundred feet from an Eastern Air Transport airplane as it neared the city of Charleston. King was traveling from Miami, Florida, to Newark, New Jersey. The trip was unremarkable until King stood up from one of the rear seats and opened an outside door. The plane lurched, and a frightened passenger saw King's hands disappearing from view. According to airport officials, although the door was not locked, due to external pressure, it is very difficult to open one during a flight. The plane was thirty miles from Charleston when King jumped. Prior to the incident, passengers noticed nothing unusual about King or his behavior. But one remembered that King had complained of a headache. Officials launched an extensive ground search but failed to locate the body.

At the time, King, a resident of Kalamazoo, Michigan, was president of Rex Paper Company. He began his career with the King Paper Company, but in 1915, he resigned that post and accepted the post of treasurer of the Rex Paper Company. John F. King, father of Merrell King, founded

Marsh along Scott Creek at the back of Edisto Beach, 1937. *Photograph WPA-PL-CH-EI-8. Courtesy of the South Caroliniana Library, University of South Carolina, Columbia.*

the Rex Paper Company. The elder king died in March 1922 and left an estate valued at $201,000. His will named his son Merrell as trustee of his estate and his stock in the Rex Paper Company. John F. King also left a widow and a daughter. On March 30, 1922, the board of directors named Merrell B. King as general manager of the company. According to the *Paper Trade Journal*, at the time, King was the "youngest paper mill executive in the Kalamazoo valley district." In 1919, King married Helen Ralston, who survived him.

Months after his disappearance, King's body was found in the marshes of the Edisto River. Authorities were able to identify the body from papers found nearby. King's body was returned to Michigan for burial. What triggered King's bizarre departure remains a mystery.

MISADVENTURE AT SEA

In 1950, several New Yorkers came to Seabrook Island for fishing and relaxation. On a fateful day in November, Edith Ecker, Joseph B. Rogers, James Merrill Herd Jr. and Peter C. Morris embarked on a fishing outing. Ecker (age fifty-two), related to former French president Raymond Poincare, was the second wife of Frederick H. Ecker (age eighty-three). Poincare served as president of France during World War I. The Eckers lived on Park Avenue

Frederick Ecker, president of Metropolitan Insurance Company. Ecker's wife, Edith, drowned during a fishing trip. Later, her body was found in the marshes of Edisto Island. *Harris & Ewing, photographer. Courtesy of Library of Congress, Prints & Photographs Division, LC-H22-D-5820.*

in New York City. Frederick Ecker was president of the Metropolitan Life Insurance Company. He began as an office boy and rose to the presidency. Rogers was a New York real estate broker, and Herd (age thirty-nine) was head of a theatrical company in New York. Peter C. Morris worked at the Seabrook estate.

Unfortunately, their craft swamped in heavy waves, and the four fell into the water. Four hours later, a trawler miraculously rescued Rogers and Morris. The next day, an air search crew spotted the body of Edith Ecker, life jacket in place. She was lying facedown on an Edisto beach. Currents had carried her body fifteen miles south of the accident. Frederick Ecker had his wife's body returned to New York City for burial. The body of her companion Herd was never found.

Scandals and Schemes

S muggling is an old and persistent problem. The United States is particularly vulnerable on all four coasts: the Atlantic, Great Lakes, Gulf and Pacific. Yet historically, according to William R. Wells II, the southeastern coast has been the "greatest target" for smugglers. The southeastern United States is riddled with bays, harbors, creeks and rivers—natural highways providing access many miles inland.

Steamboat Landing, Edisto Island, July 2013. The creeks and landings of Edisto were essential to trade and commerce but also made the island vulnerable to raids. *Terry Helsley, photographer.*

South Carolina, with its inviting waterways, has always been attractive to smugglers. Pirates preyed on Carolina commerce until 1718, when Colonel William Rhett captured Stede Bonnet. After their trial, authorities hanged the gentleman pirate and his associates at White Point in Charleston. The islands of the South Carolina Lowcountry, including Edisto, were particularly attractive to privateers, illegal slavers and blockade runners. Folk stories of buried treasure persist on Edisto. During the 1920s, according to Clara Puckette, bootleggers operated on Big Bay during Prohibition. So it is perhaps not surprising that in the 1970s, Edisto residents were involved in marijuana smuggling.

DRUG SMUGGLING

In 1977, authorities captured five young men on the beach. The men had a sailboat loaded with marijuana from Colombia, South America. In addition, on May 21, 1977, authorities raided a cabin cruiser, a forty-three-foot sloop and a motel room. They seized almost three tons of marijuana with an estimated street value of $2 million and arrested eight people. In 1978, a drug bust on Edisto Island captured about sixteen tons of marijuana, one of the largest drug busts in Charleston County history.

Shrimp boat, December 2013. *Terry Helsley, photographer.*

According to the *Spartanburg Herald Journal,* in November 1980, law enforcement officers arrested twenty-one men and seized two boats, four trucks and a large quantity of marijuana. At that time, some considered this seizure "the largest drug bust in South Carolina." Acting on a confidential tip, three Colleton County sheriff's deputies went to a boat landing on the Edisto River near Bennett's Point. There, the deputies spotted a tractor-trailer, "staked out the area and called for assistance." As the officers watched, men unloaded marijuana from two shrimp trawlers. The unloaders then used a conveyor belt to move the drugs into the two tractor-trailers.

As a result, authorities arrested five suspects and seized four vehicles. In addition, United States Customs agents arrested sixteen additional suspects on trawlers. Several of those arrested were armed and carried large amounts of cash. Sheriff John Seigler stated that although his department did "not have the exact tonnage, we feel this probably was the biggest pot bust in South Carolina history." But records were made to be broken.

Operation Jackpot

During the first administration of President Ronald Reagan, federal authorities launched a so-called war on drugs. Henry Dargan McMaster became United States attorney for the District of South Carolina in 1981. After taking office, McMaster focused on the "drug problem." He organized a task force with representatives from five different federal agencies, including the Internal Revenue Service, United States Customs, Federal Bureau of Investigation and Drug Enforcement Administration, to tackle drug smuggling in the state. Between 1983 and 1986, the task force convicted more than one hundred marijuana smugglers. McMaster's task force was one of the first to exploit federal civil forfeiture legislation to combat the drug trade. Under recently approved legislation, federal agents seized smugglers' assets, including vehicles, houses, boats and bank deposits. As a result of Operation Jackpot, the task force prosecuted four smuggling rings in South Carolina.

Henry D. McMaster graduated from the University of South Carolina Law School and served as legislative assistant for United States senator Strom Thurmond of South Carolina. Elected South Carolina attorney general, McMaster served from 2003 to 2011. He was also the unsuccessful Republican candidate for the United States Senate in 1986 and for the Republican gubernatorial nomination in 2010.

Henry Dargan McMaster was the United States attorney who oversaw the prosecution of the Jackpot drug cases in South Carolina. Nominated by Senator Strom Thurmond, McMaster became U.S. attorney in 1981. *Courtesy of South Carolina Political Collections, Hollings Special Collections Library, University of South Carolina.*

Part of the task force net snared Cleveland "Skip" Sanders. Sanders, according to Jason Ryan, had access to a special asset. His grandmother, Ella M. Seabrook, owned a 325-acre plantation on Edisto Island. More importantly for subsequent events, West Bank Plantation boasted the remnants of a deep-water dock and easy access to the Atlantic Ocean via the North Edisto River. A secluded location with deep-water access was a smuggler's dream, and Sanders was not the first to see the financial potential of the site. Since at least 1973, smugglers had been exploiting the property's location. Seeking to profit from his good fortune, Sanders began to sell one-night leases to drug smugglers. The money was good, and the risk for Sanders was limited.

In Charleston, Sanders connected with drug masterminds Barry Foy and Tom Rhoad. In 1979, Foy and Rhoad landed eight thousand pounds of marijuana on Edisto Island. This was only one of many successful operations—testimony, per Ryan, to the sophisticated planning of these "gentlemen" smugglers. Sanders purchased radar and other screening devices to guarantee the safety of drug activities on Edisto Island and also acquired radios to communicate with his spotters, who were on the lookout for law enforcement vehicles driving onto the island, and with the actual drug operatives supervising the unloading and reloading of shipments. In late 1981, his planning came to naught. Customs officials intercepted watercraft in the North Edisto River, and law enforcement converged on the West Bank landing just as the marijuana cargo was being uploaded onto several vans. Despite their efforts, some smugglers escaped, and a number of key personnel were not apprehended until much later. Officers found Sanders in his grandmother's house.

Convicted for his role in the smuggling operation, Sanders, who grew up in Beaufort, was sentenced to five years for each of two counts (sentences to run consecutively) and five additional years for each of two other counts (sentences to run concurrently). In addition, the court sentenced him to twenty-five years of parole. In 1985, Sanders and other defendants appealed their convictions. Specifically, Sanders appealed on two of the four counts, alleging that "as an off-loader, he could not be convicted of conspiracy to import." The Eleventh District Appeals Court affirmed Sanders's convictions, ruling: "To be found guilty a defendant needs not have knowledge of all the details of the conspiracy, and may only play a minor role in the total operation."

Trouble in Paradise

Edisto also figured in another major South Carolina scandal. This one involved United States congressman John Wilson Jenrette Jr. The charismatic Jenrette was a political star, wildly popular in South Carolina's Sixth Congressional District. A descendant of Huguenot immigrants, Jenrette was one of the top-ranking victims of the FBI's Abscam investigation. Jenrette, a native of Conway, South Carolina, served in the United States House of Representatives from November 5, 1975, until his resignation on December 10, 1980. At the time of the scandal, Jenrette and his beautiful wife, Rita Carpenter Jenrette, appeared prominently on the Washington, D.C. social scene.

After their divorce, Rita Jenrette wrote *My Capital Secrets*, a book about her life with the congressman. The 1981 memoir was billed as an exposé of "all the bizarre things that really happen in Washington." She opened her book with the events of Saturday, February 2, 1980—a day, according to Rita Jenrette, when life with the congressman went terribly wrong. Having just weathered accusations of drug smuggling and fraudulent land deals, the Jenrettes were relaxing at their District of Columbia home when two FBI

JENRETTE, John Wilson, Jr. (1975-81), Democrat; Lawyer and Businessman; residing at North Myrtle Beach; *b.* May 19, 1936 at Conway; *s.* John Wilson and Mary (Herring) Jenrette of Loris; *g.* Wofford Coll.; A.B., 1958; Univ. of S. C., LL.B., 1962; Sept. 10, 1976 *m.* Rita Carpenter of Austin, Tex.; 2 children, Mary Elizabeth & Harold Hampton; Atty. & City Judge for Ocean Drive Beach; Member, Official Bd. & former Chm., Finance Com. Trinity Methodist Church; Chamber of Commerce; Jaycees; Lions Club; (nominated for ten Outstanding Young Men of America); Served as Page in S. C. Senate, 1959; & as Clerk, Finance Com., 1960; at USC: Economic Research Dept., June-Nov. 1960; Pres., Student Bar Assn., 1961; Member Honor Bd., School of Law; Class Off., 3 yrs. at Wofford Coll.; Member, S. C. Huguenot Soc.; Kappa Sigma Frat.; Amer., S. C., & Co. Bar Assns.; Amer. Trial Lawyers Assn.; S. E. Forestry Advisory Bd.; Atty., N. Myrtle Beach; recipient of S. C. Municipal Assn. Distinguished Service Award, 1966; Member Steering Com. Urban Affrs. Study Com. & V.-Chm., Local Fiscal Problem Sub-Com., Sou. Council of State Govt.; former Commanding Off. Co. "A", 263rd Armor, SCNG, Myrtle Beach with rank of Capt.; Major, USAF Reserve; Military Service: Active Duty, Co. A, 18th Bn., 1st Training Regiment, 1959; Member S. C. House of Representatives, 1965-72; Elected to 94th Congress, Nov. 5, 1974, serving continuously since.

South Carolina Offices: 356 West Baroody St., Florence, Tel. 665-0341, 665-0343; Horry Co. Courthouse, Conway, Tel. 248-6247.

Entry for John W. Jenrette Jr., 1980 South Carolina Legislative Manual. Courtesy of South Carolina Department of Archives and History.

agents paid a surprise visit. The phone rang, and reporters gathered at their door. The Abscam story was front-page news.

Rita Jenrette, a native of San Antonio, Texas, was a model and political researcher when she married Jenrette in 1976. Although she testified in her husband's defense, following his conviction, she and John separated and divorced in 1981. She is also an author, actress and real estate agent. She appeared in *Playboy* twice. According to Al Kamen of the *Washington Post*, in 2009, she married Prince Nicolo Boncompagni Ludovisi and now lives in Italy.

ORISTO

In addition to his political life, Jenrette was also a businessman with a wide range of commercial interests. One of these concerned the Oristo development on Edisto Beach. As background, in 1975, the Town of Edisto Beach left Charleston County and joined Colleton County. The Oristo development began in the early 1970s. Henry S. Lybrand, former Edisto Beach mayor (Sea Island Resorts, Inc.), purchased four hundred acres on the

The golf course with lagoon and palmettos, Wyndham Resort, December 2013. Prior to his Abscam conviction, Congressman Jenrette developed and sold time shares near the golf course. *Terry Helsley, photographer.*

southern end of Edisto. After the purchase, Lybrand developed, according to the *News & Courier*, a "championship golf course." Unfortunately, the course opened in 1974 during a recession. Consequently, the developers sold about one hundred acres to Ruscon Corporation and turned over the remaining acreage to First Federal Savings & Loan in Charleston.

As a result, for a number of years, a subsidiary of First Federal operated the golf course and facilities such as the tennis court and restaurant and constructed "residential units." Then in 1978, First Federal sold Oristo to Jenrette and his partner, C.L. Fielden. That year, Jenrette and Fielden announced that they would develop Club Oristo and build condominiums around the Oristo golf course on Edisto. Afterward, they sold four town houses in the development to investors. In turn, the investors permitted the developers to use the town houses in a "time sharing plan." The sales pitch was inviting—one week, one unit, twenty-year lease for only $3,000. Reportedly, the investors/purchasers (primarily South Carolinians) were also guaranteed reduced rates for golf, tennis and other amenities. Regrettably for the marketers and the investors, the time-share plan unraveled. Consequently, "88 families" had little but "a piece of paper to show for their investment."

The situation aroused concerns, and in April 1980, the South Carolina Real Estate Commission and the South Carolina attorney general investigated. They charged Jenrette and Fielden with violating the state's "vacation time share act." As a result, a receiver, William F. Rivers, was appointed to manage the property. On May 14, Judge Donald A. Fanning instructed the receiver to seize the properties and prepare a report listing the assets and liabilities of the Jenrette/Fielden partnership. In addition, the court asked Rivers to manage the property and develop a proposal for the future of the development. Consequently, the receiver reported the partnership had liabilities of $30,000 to $50,000 and assets of only $5,000.

Facing such negative publicity, Oristo launched an advertising campaign featuring the golf course. In June 1980, First Federal began building three-story villas around the golf course. According to Rivers, while the cost at the time of managing Oristo exceeded revenues, he predicted that, in time, the development would be highly profitable.

According to the *Spartanburg Herald*, Jenrette was charged with conspiracy and bribery in the United States court. From testimony in the court, in late November 1979, the savings and loan association sent Jenrette a letter "demanding $51,000 payment on the Oristo golf-course condominium project on Edisto Island" or he would face foreclosure. Desiring to save his Oristo development, Jenrette needed a cash infusion. This situation made him vulnerable to a federal sting operation known as Abscam.

ABSCAM

In the late 1970s and early 1980s, Abscam was a sting operation run by the Federal Bureau of Investigation. In 2013, the movie *American Hustle* incorporated aspects of the Abscam investigation and the career of the convicted con man, Melvin "Mel" Weinberg, who orchestrated the hustle to avoid prison. At first, the investigation focused on trade in stolen property. But in time, the operation shifted to public corruption. FBI agents videotaped local and national politicians accepting bribes from fake sheiks. The cardboard oil magnates allegedly wanted investment opportunities for their oil profits and political favors. As a result of the sting, courts convicted one United States senator; six members of the United States House of Representatives; one member of the New Jersey State Senate; members of the Philadelphia City Council; the mayor of Camden, New Jersey; and several federal officials.

Congressman John Jenrette, major investor in Oristo condominium time shares on Edisto Island. *Courtesy of South Carolina Political Collections, Hollings Special Collections Library, University of South Carolina.*

As a result of these convictions, the House and Senate held hearings, raised issues about entrapment and questioned the FBI's use of its paid informant, a convicted con man. Despite the videotapes, there were many appeals but no reversals. Even today, legal questions remain.

Federal agents charged Jenrette with accepting a bribe to assist several Arabs with residency and immigration issues. According to Rita Jenrette, "The videotapes were damning." The tapes showed Jenrette meeting with agents and sheiks and allegedly accepting money. To Jenrette's wife, the situation was a "set-up." During the Abscam trial, defense attorney Kenneth M. Robinson asked Jenrette, "If you applied any of the money [offered by FBI agent Amoroso], could you have saved Oristo?" "I could have saved Oristo," replied Jenrette. In other words, Jenrette's attorney argued that without his commitment to the Oristo project, his client would never have accepted the Abscam bribe.

In addition, Jenrette's defense team alleged that the Justice Department had targeted the congressman. They cited the record of Justice Department investigations of Jenrette for marijuana smuggling, his Heritage Shores land development and his congressional office's use of mail and telephone privileges. None of these earlier investigations produced an indictment. Alleged entrapment and persecution were persistent themes in many of the Abscam trials.

As part of the Abscam prosecutions, on October 7, 1980, after a trial that lasted twenty-two days, the jury found Jenrette and his co-defendant, John Stone, guilty of all charges, including accepting a bribe of $50,000.

According to his wife, Jenrette "lowered his head and wept." After his conviction, Jenrette and his attorney appeared before a committee of the House of Representatives. On December 10, 1980, the committee held sanction hearings. Jenrette appeared and submitted his resignation from the House. At that point, the committee ended its proceedings.

Subsequently, Jenrette served time in federal prison. Later, he attempted to reclaim his political career but lost his bid for reelection. Then in April 1988, according to the *Augusta Chronicle*, the Edisto scandal resurfaced. South Carolina attorney general Travis Medlock was directing a settlement of a civil dispute involving Jenrette, Fielden and the Club Oristo Development. In 1981, the court had ordered the partners to repay over $100,000 to ninety-five investors in the time-share development; such payments were not made. In addition, there were other judgments against Jenrette. In time, legal issues behind him, former congressman Jenrette resumed his life.

Epilogue

"Ripples and Waves"

S ince Cain killed Abel, the history of mankind has been a long litany of man's inhumanity to man. Wickedness is alive and well. Only the names and circumstances change. In the 1920s, a youthful island resident killed another young man, possibly in an altercation. The accused alleged self-defense and served time for manslaughter. In 1945, as World War II ended, according to the *Charleston Evening Post*, authorities arrested an Edisto Island resident for theft. The accused had a ten-year career that included twenty-

The Pit, a nightclub, State Highway 174, Edisto Island, December 2013. *Terry Helsley, photographer.*

Sea oats, Edisto Beach, December 2012. *Jacob Helsley, photographer.*

seven thefts and house break-ins. In 1935, he embarked on his career of crime by stealing a bicycle, but by 1945, he had progressed to automobile theft. In September 1945, he pleaded guilty to six counts of housebreaking and theft. The long-suffering judge commented on the defendant's "reputation for stealing" and warned him not to try to "steal the truck from the prison."

In recent years, Edisto has seen domestic violence and death, gun violence at the Pit Club, suspected arson and the unusual deaths of two visitors in a hot tub.

For over three centuries, privateers, pirates, smugglers and military gunboats have plied the waterways of Edisto. Death and disappointment have lurked beneath the live oaks festooned with Spanish moss. A changing cast of characters enters and exits this unique corner of the world. Beneath the wild beauty lurk the songs of slaves, the crack of pistols, the secret canker of unresolved crime and the dark secrets of the human heart.

Selected Bibliography

Connor, Amy Sadler, and Sheila Lane Beardsley. *Edisto Island: A Family Affair.* Dover, NH: Arcadia Publishing, 1998.

Lindsay, Nick. *And I'm Glad: An Oral History of Edisto Island.* Charleston, SC: Tempus Publishing, Inc., 2000.

Mikell, I. Jenkins. *Rumbling of the Chariot Wheels: Doings and Misdoings in the Barefooted Period of a Boy's Life on a Southern Plantation.* Columbia, SC, 1923. Reprint, 2007.

Murray, Chalmers S. *Turn Backward O Time in Your Flight: A Reminiscence of Growing Up on Edisto Island.* Edisto Island, SC: Edisto Island Historic Preservation Society, 2000.

Puckette, Clara Childs. *Edisto: A Sea Island Principality.* Edisto Island, SC: Edisto Island Historic Preservation Society, 2004. Originally published 1978.

Spencer, Charles. *Edisto Island 1663 to 1860: Wild Eden to Cotton Aristocracy.* Charleston, SC: The History Press, 2008.

———. *Edisto Island 1861 to 2006: Ruin, Recovery and Rebirth.* Charleston, SC: The History Press, 2008.

Wright, Cantey. *Edisto: A Guide to Life on the Island.* Charleston, SC: The History Press, 2006.

The Edisto Historical Museum preserves the history of Edisto Island, December 2013. *Terry Helsley, photographer.*

Index

About the Author

Alexia Jones Helsley has a special love for the South Carolina Lowcountry. She grew up in Beaufort, and for many years, she and her family have spent delightful weeks at Edisto. Helsley, a historian and archivist, teaches South Carolina history at the University of South Carolina–

The author (left) and her family at the Old Post Office Restaurant, July 2013.

Aiken. Recipient of the Governor's Archives Award, she also serves as chair of the Old Exchange Building Commission. *Wicked Edisto* is her third title in the "Wicked" series, following *Wicked Beaufort* and *Wicked Columbia*.